CONTENTS

"I will give you the . . . riches stored in secret places" (Isa. 45:3).

RICHES STORED
in
SECRET PLACES

A Devotional Guide for Those Who Hunger After the Deep Things of God

Jennifer Kennedy Dean

New Hope
Birmingham, Alabama

New Hope
P. O. Box 12065
Birmingham, AL 35202-2065

Dewey Decimal Classification: 248.3
Subject Headings: DEVOTIONAL EXERCISES
SPIRITUAL LIFE
MEDITATIONS

Cover design by Steve Diggs & Friends Advertising/Public Relations

ISBN: 1-56309-203-4
N974109•0397•5M1

GETTING STARTED

I think I know why you are reading this book. I think the title—which describes my own longing to move deeper into the Spirit-led life—describes your longing. I think you are hungry for the "deep and hidden things" (Dan. 2:22) that you know are available in God's Word. Just like I am, you are hungry for "all truth" (John 16:13). That truth for which we hunger cannot be explained or taught. It must be revealed by the Spirit of God.

Jesus asked the Father to reveal truth to you and to me. He prayed that the Father would use the truth hidden in His Word to make us holy. "'Sanctify them by the truth; your word is truth'" (John 17:17). The Father always hears and answers the Son (John 11:41). As you learn how to find the riches stored in secret places, you will experience the Father's answer to the Son's prayer.

The wonderful, rich, consecrating truth in God's Word is not sitting on the surface to be skimmed off by the casual observer. It is buried, and must be mined like gold or silver.

"If you call out for insight and cry aloud for understanding, and if you look for it as for silver and search for it as for hidden treasure, then you will understand the fear of the Lord and find the knowledge of God. For the Lord gives wisdom, and from his mouth come knowledge and understanding" (Prov. 2:3–6).

The treasures of the kingdom are hidden: "Christ, in whom are hidden all the treasures of wisdom and knowledge" (Col. 2:3). Why is the deep truth hidden? Why can't the

1

treasures of wisdom and knowledge be readily accessible to any person's intellect?

God has deliberately hidden deep truth so that the Spirit of truth can disclose it. "'For whatever is hidden is meant to be disclosed, and whatever is concealed is meant to be brought out into the open'" (Mark 4:22). The truths of God's Word are buried for one purpose—so that you and I can find them.

In the process of revealing "deep and hidden things," God reinforces in His children the knowledge that we are totally dependent upon Him. Left to our own devices, we will never see any deeper than the surface. Our understanding of the truth comes directly and only from Him. In the course of learning directly from Him, intimacy is strengthened and enriched. Our hunger, our longing, is really for Him.

"We might have expected, we may think we should have preferred, an unrefracted light giving us ultimate truth in systematic form—something we could have tabulated and memorised and relied on like a multiplication table. . . . God must have done what is best, this is best, therefore God has done this.

"It may be indispensable that Our Lord's teaching, by its elusiveness (to our systematising intellect), should demand a response from the whole man, should make it so clear that there is no question of learning a subject but of steeping ourselves in a Personality."[1]

God has a loving and productive purpose for hiding and then revealing truth. As He leads you into the depths of His Word, you will learn to recognize His voice. You will become acquainted with His presence. The intimacy you will build over time creates confidence. God's voice will become so familiar to you that you will be able to discern between His voice and other voices.

My sons play baseball. They play on teams of boys their own age and size who all wear identical uniforms. When they are on the ball field and too far away to see faces or uniform numbers, I still have no difficulty picking out my sons. Instinctively, I recognize their stances or their mannerisms. I don't recognize anyone else's sons by such subtle clues, even though I know them well. Knowing someone well and knowing someone intimately are two different things. The more intimately we know the Father, the more easily we will recognize Him.

"It is the glory of God to conceal a matter; to search out a matter is the glory of kings" (Prov. 25:2). Because we have to look to Him for truth, searching it out draws us closer to His heart. At His feet, in His presence, we discover the glory that is to be ours.

The Spirit Unlocks the Kingdom Secrets

The truth is encrypted in God's Word. *Encrypt* is a computer word. It means "to convert plain text into unintelligible form by means of a code." Once text has been encrypted, any person who does not have the correct password will only see garbled text. Only those specially designated individuals who have been given the password can read encrypted information. The password is the key that unlocks the secrets in an encrypted document. Enter the password and the unintelligible text becomes plain text. The truth in God's Word is encrypted and only the children of the kingdom have the key.

"'The secret of the kingdom of God has been given to you. But to those on the outside everything is said in parables so that, 'they may be ever seeing, but never perceiving, and ever hearing but never understanding'" (Mark 4:11–12).

Do you see? You have been given the key that unlocks the kingdom's secrets. The Spirit, working directly in your mind and understanding, discloses deeper levels of truth. First Corinthians 2:12 tells you that God has given you His Spirit for this purpose: "that [you] might understand what God has freely given [you]." Because you have the Holy Spirit, you can understand what the human intellect alone is unable to comprehend. The encrypted truth will become plain to you.

The full, substantive, mature truth is hidden from the world to be revealed to those in whom the Spirit dwells. The Spirit-led life is the continual and progressive apprehension of deeper and deeper levels of truth. "'Call to me and I will answer you and tell you great and unsearchable things you do not know'" (Jer. 33:3). He will tell you truths that are beyond the ordinary (great) and inaccessible (unsearchable). The secrets of the kingdom are for the heirs of the kingdom.

Riches Stored in Secret Places

This book is about discovering deep truth by means of the Spirit's revelation. It is about learning how to listen to God's voice in His Word. "'He who belongs to God hears what God says'" (John 8:47). This book is about receiving from God the riches He has stored in secret places.

How to Use This Book

In order to use this book effectively, you will need to commit time every day. This is not a Scripture memory program. As you work through this devotional book, you will practice the methods of meditation and contemplative prayer that I have developed over the years of soaking myself in the Word of God. These methods have been helpful to me, so I believe that they will be helpful to you. Some exercises you may spend two days on; others you may do two in one day. You might skip weekend days. Don't feel bound by rules. Find the way that works for you. Develop consistency and discipline, but don't take this on as a burdensome task.

Each week you will ask the Spirit to reveal the layers of truth in a passage of Scripture. I will share some thoughts with you about that Scripture, then I will give you suggestions about how to meditate on it and pray through it. You will be looking at the same Scripture passage each day for a week at a time, but from slightly different angles. You will discover the prism effect: When you look at a passage of Scripture from various angles, you will see the Light being disseminated with different intensities and shadings. You will find that new understanding emerges and is built into your life line by line and precept by precept. You will find dimensions of truth you have never recognized before.

Each day you will have specific instructions to help you incorporate meditation and contemplation into your praying. Throughout the week you will be processing what you are discovering. In the intial weeks I will give you detailed guidance. Then I will taper off as you begin to see how to use the meditation methods.

If you want to use this book with small groups, Bible study classes, prayer partners, or in one-on-one mentoring relationships, you will find helpful suggestions beginning on page 157.

The Format
During experience 1, you will read through the day's Scripture and the devotional/study comments. Keep in mind that you are listening to God, Who has wakened your longing and has sensitized your spirit ears. (Read Isa. 50:4*b*.)

Ask God now what time He has set aside for you and Him to tryst during the day. Write it down as your commitment. Ask Him to call you to Him each day.

As often as possible, the time each day that I will be focusing on God's voice is _____.

Here's how the week will progress:
EXPERIENCE 1: Read through the Scripture and devotional thoughts. Go slowly. Any time a thought captures your attention, stop and reread it. Underline it. Let it soak in. Next, work through the reflection questions. The purpose of these questions is to prompt you to put truth into the setting of your own life, which helps solidify your thoughts. These are not questions meant to challenge your intellect.

EXPERIENCE 2: Take the Scripture passage apart and look at each piece separately. Write out each phrase. Beside it, write your own sense of what that phrase is saying to you. Pay particular attention to words like *if. . . then, so that, because, therefore, and, but,* and *when.* Underline or circle these words and consider how they reveal connections or cause-and-effect relationships.

During this meditative exercise, listen for the Holy Spirit to prompt you by bringing to mind other Scripture verses or passages that shed more light on any phrase in this passage. Write them down. Next, put the pieces back together. From your meditation, paraphrase the Scripture passage.

While you are doing this meditative exercise, also be aware of any word, phrase, or concept that creates a picture in your mind. God designed our brains so that they work by turning words, phrases, and thoughts into mental images. If I were to say the word *tree,* your mind would immediately "see" a tree. God speaks to that feature of your brain by using visual language in His Word. If a phrase or a concept creates a picture or scene in your mind, sketch it out or describe it. You don't have to be a great artist. These drawings are, once again, to explore truth from different angles and to solidify your thoughts.

EXPERIENCE 3: I want to introduce you to what I call my "Jeopardy" method of meditating. "Jeopardy" is a popular game in which the player, having been given the answer, must supply the question. Look at the Scripture and ask yourself: "What questions does this passage answer?" List the questions and the answers. I usually go phrase by phrase or thought by thought. When you are finished, look back through your list. You will see new angles to the truth.

EXPERIENCE 4: As you have meditated this week, what has God said to you? Remember that He wants to speak to you directly—to call you by name. Write down your name, then write what you are hearing God say. For example, I might write, *Darling Jennifer,* or *Beloved Daughter,* or *Apple of My*

Eye, or *Highly Favored One* or any endearment I hear Him use toward me. Then I would write out His personal Word to me from my meditations. Take time on this morning to enjoy His passionate, tender love for you. Even when His word to you is a word of correction or reproof, it is loving and gentle.

EXPERIENCE 5: Write your honest, heartfelt response to God. In your private time with Him, learn to use terms of endearment. Call Him *My Greatest Love, Father* like Jesus did. Call Him *Beloved,* or *My Comfort.* Learn to be lovingly intimate and at ease with Him.

Sometimes your response may be loving and faith-filled. Sometimes it may be confusion, or doubt, or even anger and frustration. Be honest. God is not fragile. His love for you is absolutely steadfast, immovable, never wavering. You can trust Him to love you unconditionally.

EXPERIENCE 6: Based on your meditations this week, what assurances or promises has God made you in His Word? Write them down. Pray these promises as the Holy Spirit applies them to people or situations He has assigned you for intercession. Write the name or situation next to the promise. Date it. Think of this exercise as harvesting each promise and praying it into a specific life or situation. When the Father says in His Word that all of His promises are already yes in Christ, that causes me to picture a field of ripe and ready grain. The grain is ready to harvest. When we pray based on God's promises, we are harvesting those promises. You do not have to watch to see if God will fulfill His Word. Instead, watch to see how God is fulfilling His Word.

EXPERIENCE 7: Based on your listening to God, write out faith statements for your life. Faith statements are declarative statements that put into words that which without seeing you know to be true. "Faith is being certain of what you do not see" (Heb. 11:1). This provides you with the basis for praise, worship, and adoration. Spend your contemplative time today praising and worshiping God the Father, God the Son, and God the Spirit.

Inwardly, privately, worship with abandon. Sing to Him. Applaud Him. Kiss His hands. Anoint His feet. Shout, "Hosanna!" Bow before Him. Worship Him without self-consciousness. All this can be done in your mind, what Thomas R. Kelly refers to as "the secret sanctuary."[2]

During each experience, you will process and solidify what you have gleaned from the Scripture by using the meditative exercises in this book. This book can be the beginning of a spiritual journal. Let your experience with this book be the starting point for a wonderful pilgrimage in the Spirit.

Let the Spirit Progressively Unfold the Truth

Your week of meditating on a passage will be only the beginning. You will not discover all the riches stored there in a week. With these methods, you will be depositing God's Word in your mind so that the Spirit can be making withdrawals from it and applying it to your situations. As you continue to marinate your life in His truth, the Spirit will make connections between passages. You will notice a thread of truth running through the Word. At an unexpected moment, God will shine a search light on a truth from a Scripture you thought you had already mined. You will see something clearly that you had not noticed or put together before. It will be so plain that you will wonder how it escaped you. What has been hidden is suddenly revealed. What has been encrypted is suddenly made plain.

My Prayer for All Readers

I pray that the Lord will confide in you and make His covenant promises understood by you. I pray that you will respond to His Word so that He will pour out His heart to you and cause you to understand His thoughts. My prayer for you is based on Psalm 25:14: "The Lord confides in those who fear him, he makes his covenant known to them"; and Proverbs 1:23: "If you had responded to my rebuke, I would have poured out my heart to you and made my thoughts known to you."

You are prayed for! Begin using this book with the assurance that God Himself will teach you. The prayer I prayed for you will be abundantly answered in your life. How do I know that? Because I have God's Word on it.

"This is the assurance we have in approaching God: that if we ask anything according to his will, he hears us. And if we know that he hears us—whatever we ask—we know that we have what we asked of him" (1 John 5:14–15).

[1]C. S. Lewis, *Reflections on the Psalms* (San Diego: Harcourt Brace and Company, 1986), 112–14.
[2]Thomas R. Kelly, *A Testament of Devotion* (New York: Harper and Row, Publishers, 1941), 43.

FINDING HIDDEN RICHES

Experience 1

"'No eye has seen, no ear has heard, no mind has conceived what God has prepared for those who love him'—but God has revealed it to us by his Spirit. The Spirit searches all things, even the deep things of God" (1 Cor. 2:9–10). (Focal passage: 1 Cor. 2:6–16)

God has everything you need prepared for you. Every answer to every need is ready and waiting. "And my God will meet all your needs according to his glorious riches in Christ Jesus" (Phil. 4:19). God has already said yes. "No matter how many promises God has made, they are 'Yes' in Christ" (2 Cor. 1:20). Everything you need for life or for godliness is freely available to you. Second Peter 1:3 assures you that "His divine power has given us everything we need for life (material needs) and godliness (spiritual needs) through our knowledge of him who called us by his own glory and goodness." (Parenthetical expressions added for clarification.)

When you know that every need has already been met, then you can experience the peace to which God calls you. You do not need to have anxiety about anything. Instead, you can trust Him for His provision. When you understand that God has everything prepared and waiting for you and that it comes into your life by means of prayer, then it makes sense to wrap your petitions in thanksgiving. "Do not be anxious about anything, but in everything, by prayer and petition, with thanksgiving, present your requests to God" (Phil. 4:6).

You don't have to wait until you see the answer with your senses to know that you possess it. "If we know that he hears us . . . we know that we have what we asked of him" (1 John 5:15). As soon as you present Him your need, the supply is assured. He always meets your needs. How He meets those needs is up to Him.

When I was a college student, I didn't pay my own bills. My dad paid them. Once I dropped a bill in the mail to him, I never worried about it. In my mind, it became his bill immediately. I cast all my debts on Dad and left them there. Why? Because he had promised to pay my bills, I knew that he had everything I needed available for me and with my best interest at heart, he always released it on my behalf when I asked.

That's how it is with your heavenly Father. He is your provider. "Cast your cares on the Lord and he will sustain you" (Psalm 55:22). Once you bring God your request, consider that need met. Don't focus on the need; instead focus on the supply. Your role is to take the need to your Father. As you live in an obedient and trustful relationship with Him, you will have no reason to be anxious and can be expectant instead. The psalmist prays: "Morning by morning, O Lord, you hear my voice; morning by morning I lay my requests before you and wait in expectation" (Psalm 5:3). "The one who calls you is faithful and he will do it" (1 Thess. 5:24).

When anxiety knocks, refuse it entrance by expressing thanksgiving to God. When your requests are made with thanksgiving, His peace stands guard over your heart and mind.

In 1 Corinthians 2:9 (KJV), Paul refers to "the things which God hath prepared for them that love him." God has things prepared for you—things you need to know about and understand. The word translated "things" means good, profitable, useful things. Unless you know what is prepared and available for you, you will not be confident in accessing God's supply of good things by means of prayer. Unless you know what is prepared for you, you will not be able to live in uninterrupted peace and assurance.

This is why God wants you to know exactly what is available to you. However, you can't know what is available to you in the same way that you know other things. You can't know it by observing it with your eyes. You can't evaluate and measure it and describe its color and texture. You can't hear it with your ears. It does not have a certain tone or resonance that your ears will recognize as sound. You can't even imagine it or conceive of it. It would never enter your mind. The things that God has prepared for you are outside your realm of thinking. They are beyond you. You cannot depend on your imagination to discover the things God has for you.

The Spirit Reveals God's Provision

How, then, will you know the things that God has prepared for those that love Him? How can you know what God has ready for you? Those things you can't know by seeing or hearing or imagining, you can know by revelation from the Spirit. "'No eye has seen, no ear has heard, no mind has conceived . . . but God has revealed it to us by his Spirit'" (1 Cor. 2:9–10). The word *reveal* means to unveil or to uncover. It literally means to take off the cover. The Spirit will uncover the things prepared for you and expose them to your spirit eyes.

> "I keep asking that the God of our Lord Jesus Christ, the glorious Father, may give you the Spirit of wisdom and revelation, so that you may know him better. I pray also that the eyes of your heart may be enlightened in order that you may know the hope to which he has called you, the riches of his glorious inheritance in the saints, and his incomparably great power for us who believe" (Eph. 1:17–18).

How will you know His hope, His riches, and His power, all of which are available to you? When He uncovers them and shows them to the eyes of your heart, then you will know. "'The knowledge of the secrets of the kingdom of God have been given to you'" (Luke 8:10).

Imagine a beautiful painting. The artist has worked on it until it is perfect in every detail. It is his greatest achievement. He has poured himself into this work of art. Now it is finished, ready to be shown to art lovers. He invites those he knows will understand his artistic intent to an unveiling. He covers his perfect creation so that he can unveil it at exactly the right moment.

The art lovers gather. Anticipation runs high. The artist is reputed to be brilliant. As they wait, the art lovers imagine what is behind the veil. Finally, the moment arrives. All eyes are on the artist. He pulls away the veil to reveal his creation to those gathered. They are astounded at its beauty and perfection. It is more than they had imagined. They honor and applaud the artist. They eagerly anticipate his next creation.

Until the artist unveiled it, his creation was beyond sight and beyond imagination. Until the artist unveiled it, art lovers could only speculate about the true work. So it is with the Spirit's uncovering of the things God has prepared. They are beyond your imagination. They are perfect in every detail. They belong to you. You have been invited to His unveiling. What He has prepared for you is beyond all that you can ask or imagine. (Read Eph. 3:20.)

Spirit Hearing

The Spirit is the voice of God, carrying His Word to your spirit ears. Jesus said that the Spirit would lead you into all truth and would make everything about Jesus clear to you. The Spirit, indwelling you, is the revealer of deep truth. "The Spirit searches all things, even the deep things of God" (1 Cor. 2:10).

When Jesus lived in a physical body, He taught His disciples many things. He could not, however, teach them all things. Much of what He wanted to teach them had to wait. Why? Because it was deeper than their ability to comprehend.

"'I have much more to say to you, more than you can now bear. But when he, the Spirit of truth comes, he will guide you into all truth'" (John 16:12–13). Jesus explained that the

Holy Spirit would take up where He left off. The Spirit brings glory to Jesus by taking what belongs to Jesus and explaining it to you (John 16:14). The treasures of wisdom and knowledge which are hidden in Jesus are disclosed to you by the Spirit.

The Spirit will not teach you only portions of the truth. He plumbs the depths of God. He searches out the deep and hidden things in order to reveal them to you. The word *deep* means secret, unrevealed, profound, inscrutable, mysterious.

Imagine. You have access to the mysteries of God that were hidden from Moses and Elijah and Noah and Joseph and David and all the mighty men of the Old Covenant. "'I tell you that many prophets and kings wanted to see what you see but did not see it, and to hear what you hear but did not hear it'" (Luke 10:24). You can know the things into which the angels long to look (1 Peter 1:12*b*).

God Wants You to Know

God plans for you to be "filled with the knowledge of His will" (Col. 1:9 KJV). He wants you to know what you can expect of Him. He has made it clear that "everything is already yours as a gift . . . all of it is yours, and you are privileged to be in union with Christ, who is in union with God" (1 Cor. 3:21,23 *The Message*). He has bound Himself to you in covenant so that you will never have to wonder if you can count on Him. You can know, by the Spirit, what He has prepared for you. "We have not received the spirit of the world but the Spirit who is from God, that we may understand what God has freely given us" (1 Cor. 2:12).

Reflections Questions

1. Do you long to know the deep truths of God? Or are you satisfied with simple, pat answers?

2. Are you searching for a person who can hand you the deep things of God? Or are you looking to the Master Himself?

(When you are looking to God, He will often use one of His tools in the body of Christ, but He Himself will be the Source. He will bring you into contact with anyone through whom He plans to teach you.)

3. What do you feel that you know? In what area do you feel competent?

4. How did you learn the skills necessary? Did you take a class? Did you take lessons? Learn by personal experience? Learn from a mentor?

5. Can you learn the deep things of God in the same way that you learned or are learning your earthly skills?

4. How will you learn the deep things of God?

7. What are your needs and deep desires right now? List them.

8. Ask God to reveal to your understanding the needs and desires for which He has already made provision. As He does so, write down what He says. (This will unfold over time.) Ask Jesus to stand guard over your heart and mind.

Experience 2

Break the Scripture passage down into phrases. Beside each phrase, write your own sense of what that phrase means. Write down any Scripture references that the Spirit brings to your mind that would enhance or clarify the meaning of any phrase. Sketch or describe any visual thoughts.

For a few weeks, I am going to write out how I would do it. Add your own thoughts to what I have written. Remember, you are inquiring of the Spirit. Let my words serve only to help you see the thought processes involved.

(2 Cor. 2:9–10)	My thoughts	Other Scriptures
No eye has seen,	*No human eye has ever looked on or viewed from earth; I can't see with my eyes.*	2 Cor. 4:18
no ear has heard,	*No human ear has ever registered the sound of; I can't hear with my ears.*	
no mind has conceived	*No human mind has ever thought of— it is beyond my wildest imagination.*	Eph. 3:20
what God has prepared	*The good things that God has completely made ready beforehand, worked out all the details of.*	Isa. 65:24
for those who love him—	*Those who are in love with Him; those who are committed to Him in a love relationship; me.*	

but God has revealed it	*I can't learn them for myself; but—on the other hand; in contrast— God has made them knowable and available to me; God is doing the action—He is revealing.*	Jer. 33:3 Psalm 25:14
to us	*What God has available can be known by me. God is doing the revealing and I am accepting the revealing.*	
by his Spirit.	*God is revealing by means of His Spirit—He uses no other means.*	
The Spirit searches	*The Spirit knows the details of . . .*	
all things,	*everything*	John 16:12–13
even the deep things of God.	*including the unsearchable mysteries of God.*	

Restate the Scripture: *Even though no human faculty can be used to understand the unfathomable, unsearchable mysteries of God—the good things He has prepared for me—I can know those unknowable things because God has chosen to reveal them to me by His Spirit, Who indwells me.*

Visual thoughts: *I imagine myself searching for a treasure chest that I know contains everything I need. I know it exists, but I can't find it. I'm looking all over the surface of the earth. Jesus comes to me and says, "Let's dig in this very spot." We dig together until our shovels hit something solid. Jesus pulls it out, unlocks it, opens it, and hands it to me. He is as thrilled and happy to give it to me as I am to receive it from Him.*

Experience 3

What questions does this passage answer? Go through each thought in this Scripture and state the question to which it is an answer (the "Jeopardy" method). Then answer the question. Remember, the purpose of this method is not to challenge your intellect. It is simple and direct. Don't try to complicate it. It's just another way to explore the content and solidify your thoughts.

For a few weeks, I will go through this meditative exercise. Write down anything else the Spirit brings to your mind. Don't depend totally on me.

"'No eye has seen, no ear has heard, no mind has conceived what God has prepared for those who love him'—but God has revealed it to us by his Spirit. The Spirit searches all things, even the deep things of God" (1 Cor. 2:9–10).

Q: Has anyone ever seen what God has prepared?
A: No.

Q: Can what God has prepared be observed and searched out in the same way earth things are searched out?
A: No.

Q: Has anyone ever heard what God has prepared?
A: No.

Q: Can what God has prepared be learned and understood by listening with earth ears?
A: No.

Q: Has any mind ever imagined what God has prepared?
A: No.

Q: God has prepared good things for whom?
A: Those who love Him: Me.

Q: Is God in the process of preparing everything I need, or has
   He already prepared everything I need?
A: He has already prepared everything I need.

Q: When I have a need, will God have to think about it and
   decide what He will do? Or has He started answering even
   before I called?
A: He has already started answering. The answer is finished and
   waiting for me.

Q: Does God want me to be unsure of what He has prepared?
A: No. He wants me to know the things that are available to me.

Q: How will God let me know what I can count on from Him?
A: He will reveal it through His Spirit.

Q: Is there anything the Spirit doesn't know?
A: No. The Spirit knows even the deep things of God.

Q: Can I know only shallow truth?
A: No. I can know the deep things of God.

Experience 4

Write out what you are hearing God say to you as you meditate on His Word. For a few weeks, I am going to write down some of my thoughts. Please write out your own. Add your own salutation. How is God addressing you? What loving name is He using?

Dear Child:

I want you to be in My "inner circle." I long for you to know the mysteries that I reveal only to My beloved children. I want you to know My depths so that you can have perfect, uninterrupted confidence in Me. I want you to live in peace. You are secure in Me. I have wonderful, beneficial things ready for you. They are set aside and marked with your name. May I give them to you? Would you listen to My Spirit voice? Would you receive the deep truth that I want you to understand?

What worries you? Tell Me about it. Then take time to listen to Me and let Me speak My promises to you. I will give you peace and assurance. What are you lacking? Ask Me for it. Listen to Me and I will guide you into My provision.

Let Me teach you how to use the senses of your spirit so that you can know Me the way I long for you to know Me. "Open wide your mouth and I will fill it" (Psalm 81:10).

Experience 5

Write out your honest, heartfelt response to God. This week I will write out my thoughts. Add your own. Fill in the salutation. How are you going to address God in this response? At the end, after you have prayed, underline any thoughts expressed here that match yours and add your own; then sign your name.

_____:

I want to know You. I don't want anything more than to know the secrets of Your kingdom. I am hungry for You and for Your truth. I trust You completely with every need and every desire. I give them to You—they are Yours. I no longer own any need or any desire because I am turning them over to You. From now on, when I feel needs and desires, I will know that I am feeling Your needs and desires. I know that in meeting my needs and fulfilling my deepest desires and longings, You are putting Your will on the earth. I trust You. You are not working against me, but for me.

Let me understand Your ways. Fill me with the knowledge of Your will.

Forgive me for focusing my attention on the circumstances of this earth. Forgive me for opening the door to anxiety. Forgive me for thinking of Your glory in terms too small and limited. Expand my vision until it matches Yours.

I LOVE YOU,

Experience 6

What promises has God made real to you from His Word? Write them down. Beside each, write the names of those for whom you are harvesting each ripe and ready promise. Remember, the person may be you. Write the date on which you prayed it into that person's life. You might pray one promise for several people. Let the Spirit lead.

For a few weeks, I will write down my thoughts. Add your own or restate these so that they are specific to your life, your needs, your desires.

1. God will fill _____'s spiritual hunger with satisfying, solid food.
Date_____

2. God will bring _____ deeper and deeper levels of understanding.
Date_____

3. God will reveal to _____ what is prepared and waiting for _____ in the spirit realm and He will place it into _____'s life when I pray.
Date_____

4. God has only good and beneficial things prepared for _____.
Date_____

Experience 7

Write out faith statements that have taken shape during your inquiry of the Spirit. Let these be the basis of extended praise and worship. I will write out some of my thoughts. Add your own and restate these so that they are specific to your life and situation.

✝ *God will progressively reveal to me new levels of understanding.*

✝ *I can know and understand the deep things of God.*

✝ *God has wonderful things set aside and earmarked for me.*

✝ *God will reveal Himself. I need only be receptive to Him.*

✝ *God is eager to reveal to me His deep truths.*

✝ *God is generous. He will pour out His thoughts to me.*

Worship with abandon in your secret sanctuary!

A HEART LIKE HIS

Experience 1

"'I will give you a new heart and put a new spirit in you; I will remove from you your heart of stone and give you a heart of flesh. And I will put my Spirit in you and move you to follow my decrees and be careful to keep my laws'" (Ezek. 36:26). (Focal passage: Ezek. 36:22–32)

God spoke these words to Ezekiel when the Old Covenant was in effect. The Old Covenant was a covenant of promise. With these words, God promised to put a new covenant into effect—a covenant of fulfillment. You and I live under the covenant of fulfillment. What God promised in Ezekiel, He has fulfilled in us. We can translate the words *I will* as *I have*.

We hear it this way: "I have given you a new heart and have put a new spirit in you; I have removed from you your heart of stone and have given you a heart of flesh. I have put My Spirit in you and am moving you to follow my decrees and to be careful to keep my laws."

The heart is the seat of the will, the intellect, and the emotions. The "spirit" is the part of our nature that longs for God and that senses the invisible aspects of reality. It is our God-consciousness. Together, the heart and spirit make up the inner person. God tells us that when we enter into His covenant through the blood of His Son, He performs a heart transplant. The old, sick, dying heart is cut away and removed. It no longer exists. It has been replaced by a new and healthy heart. The old spirit center, the spirit center that could not be indwelt by God because of its sin stains, has been removed and replaced by a new spirit—His Spirit.

God describes the old heart as a "heart of stone." It is lifeless. It cannot receive or dispense the flow of blood. It is hardened and impenetrable. It cannot be shaped and molded. In contrast, the new heart He has given is a "heart of flesh." It pulses. It takes in and pumps out life.

The old heart is to the new heart as stone is to flesh. They are not even in the same category. The two are entirely different entities. One is dead and eroding, the other is alive and growing stronger day by day.

Heart Transplant

When a patient receives a heart transplant, what is the patient's part in the operation? Is he to give the surgeon direction? Is the surgeon looking to him for help, expecting him to be involved in the surgical procedure? Surely not. If the patient were to try to help the surgeon perform the surgery, he would only limit the surgeon and complicate the procedure. The patient is to yield himself to the work of the surgeon. The patient doesn't have to understand the intricacies of the procedure, he simply has to put himself into the surgeon's hands.

God Has Implanted His Own Heart

God describes the new covenant in terms of what He Himself will do: "I will . . . I will . . . I will." He will initiate it, He will draw it up, He will offer it, His blood will seal it, and—if we enter into it—He will perform it through us. He'll do His part and—with our yieldedness—He'll do our part.

"I will put my Spirit within you and move you to follow My decrees." He will move you to act on His will. Your body will be the instrument through which God does His will. When He took out your lifeless spirit center, He replaced it with Himself. He is within you carrying out your part of the covenant through you.

"It is God who works in you to will and to act according to his good purpose" (Phil. 2:13).

"Now to him who is able to do immeasurably more than all we ask or imagine, according to his power that is at work within us" (Eph. 3:20).

"I no longer live, but Christ lives in me" (Gal. 2:20).

"To this end I labor, struggling with all his energy, which so powerfully works in me" (Col. 1:29).

"'I will make a new covenant. . . . It will not be like the covenant I made with their forefathers . . . because they did not remain faithful to my covenant. . . . This is the covenant I will make. . . . I will put my laws in their minds and write them on their hearts" (Heb. 8:8–10).

Our only part in the New Covenant is to yield to His work in us. Our yieldedness is all He needs. As we mature in the ways of the Spirit, and as we relinquish more control of our own lives, He is able to perform His work through our willingness. Each piece of ourselves we surrender, God possesses. In those surrendered areas, His will becomes our will; we find ourselves instinctively desiring and doing His will. He moves us to do His will. If we are alert to the Spirit, we will recognize God's hand in the details and seeming coincidences of every day. We will become familiar with His nudge, which previously we had thought of as a spontaneous idea. We will recognize His transforming influence in our desires and wills, which we once thought of as changing or maturing tastes.

Even the most ordinary idea, thought, or activity is often Him moving us to do His will. When we act on what seems to be a random choice, we will often find ourselves right in the middle of the "good works, which God prepared in advance for us to do" (Eph. 2:10).

When we fully and wholeheartedly enter into the fullness of His covenant, we feel less need to struggle to search out God's will because His will searches us out. We walk continually in the flow of His will as He releases His power from our spirit center into our personalities, intellects, will, emotions, and desires. He reproduces His will in us. We begin to understand faith as rest, rather than faith as work. While our bodies are busy carrying out His will, our minds and emotions are resting in Him.

He has taken out your heart of stone and has given you a heart of flesh. He is moving you to do His will.

Reflection Questions

1. Remember a time when you "happened" to be at the right time and the right place for God's will to take effect in your life. Try to remember the seemingly trivial details that created the situation. Ask the Spirit to bring it to your remembrance.

2. Now do you see God's activity, moving you to do His will through situations that seemed unimportant at the time?

3. Are there situations in your life about which you are anxiously seeking God's will? Name them.

4. Do you believe God will act through your yieldedness?

5. Have you yielded yourself to Him in this particular decision? Write out your statement of surrender in detail.

6. Trust Him to move you to do His will. Move ahead, step-by-step, allowing Him to express His will through your yielded will. What one step do you need to take to move forward on your best understanding of His will? It may be making a phone call, or gathering preliminary information, or taking a class. It will probably be something small and simple. Step-by-step, God will open and close doors, bring you into contact with the right people, lead you to the needed information. At each step, maintain your yieldedness. You cannot anticipate the turns in the road. The road may have a different destination than you anticipated when you took the first step, but God is leading you in His way. What is the step in front of you? Write it down.

7. Are there any areas of your life through which God is unable to express His will and His power because you are maintaining ownership? Let the Spirit show the areas to you. Write it down. Tell Him, "I am willing to be made willing."

Experience 2

Today, break the passage down into phrases. Write out what each phrase is saying to you—how you are processing it in your life. Write down any Scripture references that come to mind that will expand on that concept. Draw or describe any visual thoughts. Today, I will write down some of my thoughts. Add yours, or change these to express yours.

(Ezek. 36:26)	My thoughts	Other Scriptures
I will give you	*God has taken the initiative; this relationship is His idea; He has given me what I cannot create or produce for myself.*	John 3:16 John 6:32–33
a new heart	*a clean heart; a fresh start*	Psalm 51:7 John 15:3
and put a new spirit in you;	*and put a new core in me.*	Gal. 2:20
I will remove from you your heart of stone	*He has surgically removed my fossilized, hardened, lifeless core*	Rom. 6:6
and give you a heart of flesh.	*and replaced it with a malleable, moldable, life-pumping core.*	
And I will put my Spirit in you	*He has given me Himself as my core.*	John 14:17
and move you to follow my decrees and be careful to keep my laws.	*He will do His will through me and will demonstrate His power in my life; He will transform my will and desires from within; He will make following Him instinctual.*	John 7:37–39 Phil. 2:13

Restate the Scripture: *God has performed a heart transplant on me. He has extracted and disposed of my resistant-to-Him nature and replaced it with His own Life. He is alive in me and is molding my thoughts, actions, ideas, and desires so that they conform to my new spirit center.*

Sketch or describe any visual thoughts: *I picture an artist making a plaster cast of a person's face. The artist covers the face with plaster so that the plaster will conform to the shape of the face. The plaster cast will accurately portray the person's face because it has taken on the exact shape of the face.*

The face, the living pattern for the outer expression, is the Father's Spirit life in me. The plaster cast is the outward expression of my life. It is made up of a mixture of my personality, my intellect, my instincts, and my will and desires. His Life inside me is recreating my outer being—the me the world sees.

Experience 3

Today use the "Jeopardy" method. What questions does this Scripture answer? I will write out some of my thoughts. Add your own or change mine so that they say what you want to say. My thoughts are only a guide. Let the Spirit lead you.

"'I will give you a new heart and put a new spirit in you; I will remove from you your heart of stone and give you a heart of flesh. And I will put my Spirit in you and move you to follow my decrees and be careful to keep my laws'" (Ezek. 36:26).

Q: Does God require me to transform myself?
A: No. He has given me a new heart and put a new spirit in me.

Q: Has He patched up and cleaned up my old heart?
A: No. He has taken my old heart out and replaced it with a new heart.

Q: Has He put a new heart alongside my old heart so that two spirit centers exist in me and vie for ownership?
A: No. My old core has been removed and replaced by a new core. I only have one life-pumping spirit center.

Q: Is my new heart anything like my old heart?
A: No. They are as different from each other as stone is different from flesh.

Q: Does God require me to work up the motivation to do His will and then perform it with my own energy?
A: No. He will move me to do His will.

Q: What does God need from me in order to perform a heart transplant?
A: Only my yieldedness.

Experience 4

Write down what you are hearing God say to you as you focus on His Word. Fill in the salutation. By what loving name is He calling you? Today I am writing some of my own thoughts. Add your own or restate these so that they are yours.

_____:

You are the child of My heart. I created you because I find plea-sure in you. You exist because I will you to exist. I want you to find all the joy and meaning and purpose that I have always meant for you to have. Everything I have for you is in My Son. As My life flows through Him and His life flows through you— as We make Our home in you—We are directing you in the path of joy.

I am in you. Yield to Me so that I can possess every part of you and set you free to live in My fullness. I'm the One Who is mov-ing you to do My will. I'm the One Who is changing you. I'm the One Who is motivating you. Wherever you're letting Me, I'm liv-ing through you. Come to Me. I will give you rest.

I want to show you the places inside you that are not available to Me—the places you've fenced off and are keeping as your own. I want to show you because these are places where I long to pour out My power. In maintaining your ownership, you are settling for much less that I have planned. Hand me the title deed and I will tear down the fences. I will move in. I will take possession. I will . . . I will . . . I will.

Experience 5

Write out your response to God. Rewrite my thoughts to make them yours. Add your thoughts. Trust the Spirit in you to uncover your true response. How will you address Him?

_____:

I realize that I have overlooked Your activity and mistaken it for mine. I realize that anything about me that even slightly resembles You is the result of Your work. I have done nothing and can never do anything to make myself like You. I can't change myself anymore than stone can change itself into flesh—anymore than a leopard can change its spots.

I want You to fill me, saturate me, drench me from the inside out. Take over every corner of me. Now that I have tasted Your life, I can never be satisfied with anything else. Move me to do Your will and to be careful to keep Your laws.

These are the areas of my life that I sense You asking for; I am asking You to move in and possess these areas:

Experience 6

Write out the promises God has made to you from His Word. Write the name of the person(s) for whom you are harvesting each promise.

1. God will perform His own plan. He will remove a stone heart and replace it with a flesh heart.
Date_____

2. God will put His Spirit in _____.
Date_____

3. God will move _____ to do His will.
Date_____

Experience 7

Write out the faith statements that God has implanted in you as you have listened to Him. Make this the basis of your praise and worship.

✞ *God has placed His own heart in me.*

✞ *I can instinctively live in God's will.*

✞ *God has removed my old life and my old heart from me.*

✞ *God will act through me to do His will.*

✞ *God will keep my part of the covenant by living His life in and through me.*

✞ *I live in a blood-sealed covenant with a covenant-keeping God. I can absolutely, without reservation, count on Him to keep covenant with me.*

Worship with abandon in your secret sanctuary!

THE WORD THAT SUSTAINS THE WEARY

"'He who sent me is reliable, and what I have heard from him I tell the world'. . . 'I do nothing on my own but speak just what the Father has taught me'" (John 8:26,28). (Focal passage: John 8:12–30)

"'These words you hear are not my own; they belong to the Father who sent me'" (John 14:24). (Focal passage: John 14:23–24)

I've always been accused of being exactly like my dad. People say that we are alike in looks, in temperament, in personality, in the way we process information, and in how we communicate. My two sisters, when the three of us are together, will often react to some statement of mine by looking at each other, rolling their eyes, and saying in unison, "That's Daddy talking."

They mean that I am expressing my own thoughts, but that my own thoughts are exactly like my father's. If he were present, he'd have said exactly what I said. You might say I'm speaking my father's words.

The Father Speaks Through the Son

Jesus said, "When I speak, it's really My Father talking." However, when Jesus spoke His Father's words, the connection was much deeper than my connection with my dad. His Father lived in Him. The Father, living in Jesus, did His work through the words that Jesus spoke. What kind of work did the Father do through Jesus when Jesus spoke the Father's words?

First, He performed miracles. When Jesus spoke the Father's powerful, creating, healing words, the Father worked miracles.

> "'Don't you believe that I am in the Father, and that the Father is in me? The words I say to you are not just my own. Rather, it is the Father, living in me, who is doing his work. Believe me when I say that I am in the Father and the Father is in me; or at least believe the evidence of the miracles themselves'" (John 14:10–11).

Do you see that Jesus said the Father's words do the Father's work? When He spoke the Father's words, the Father did His work. What work? In this instance, Jesus specifically pointed to the evidence of the miracles He performed. Mentally put a marker at this passage. We'll come back to it later to see how Jesus finishes this thought.

> "'I did not speak of my own accord, for the Father who sent me commanded me what to say and how to say it. I know that his command leads to eternal life. So whatever I say is just what the Father has told me to say'" (John 12:49–50).

Here, Jesus said that the Father not only told Him what to say but also told Him how to say it. In this instance Jesus said that the Father's words lead to eternal life. Remember when Peter said to Jesus, "'Lord, to whom shall we go? You have the words of eternal life'" (John 6:68)? Jesus said that He didn't have His own words, He had the Father's words. The Father had the words of eternal life. He spoke them through Jesus.

When Jesus spoke the Father's words, the Father did His work of salvation and performing miracles. When Jesus was on earth in a physical vehicle known as a body, God was on earth operating through that physical vehicle named Jesus. "For in Christ all the fullness of the Deity lives in bodily form" (Col. 2:9). God had specifically prepared a body for Jesus to inhabit (Heb. 10:5), a body through whom God would do His work.

The Son Speaks Through the Spirit

In His final days in physical form, Jesus told His disciples that He had much more to tell them, but He couldn't tell them at that time because it was more than they could comprehend. It was beyond them. It was too much for their human intellect to absorb. (Read John 16:12.) However, Jesus didn't say He would never tell them. He said He would tell them later. When would He tell them?

> "'But when he, the Spirit of truth comes, he will guide you into all truth'" (John 16:13).

Jesus calls the Holy Spirit the Spirit of truth. What is truth? Jesus said, "'I am . . . the truth'" (John 14:6). The Spirit of truth is the Spirit of Jesus. He said in John 16:25, "'Though I have been speaking figuratively, a time is coming when I will no longer use this kind of language but will tell you plainly about my Father.'" When the Spirit of truth guides you into all truth, Jesus Himself will be speaking plainly to you about the Father.

Jesus continued explaining the Spirit. He said, "'He will not speak on his own; he will speak only what he hears, and he will tell you what is yet to come'" (John 16:13). Does this remind you of Jesus' statements about Himself? Jesus said that He did not speak on His own, but spoke only what He heard from the Father. Whose words will the Spirit speak? He will voice the words of Jesus. "'He will bring glory to me by taking from what is mine and making it known to you'" (John 16:14). In other words, the Spirit will actively take hold of all that belongs to Jesus and will explain it—transmit it—to you. Eugene Peterson (in *The Message)* paraphrases this verse, "'He will take from me and deliver it to you.'"

Let me ask you a question. If your mother sends you a gift through the mail, when that gift is delivered by the mail carrier, whom do you acknowledge as the source? Not the mail carrier. She or he only delivered the gift. The person who sent the gift is the source. The mail carrier took from what belonged to your mother and delivered it to you.

When the Holy Spirit takes hold of what belongs to Jesus and transmits it to you, it is Jesus Himself speaking to you. He is the Word. The Spirit is the voice that delivers the Word. The Word and the voice are engaging in one action called speaking. Jesus is the source of everything the Spirit delivers to you.

Jesus explained further, "'All that belongs to the Father is mine. That is why I said the Spirit will take from what is mine and make it known to you'" (John 16:15). What belongs to the Father and what belongs to the Son are two ways of saying the same thing. Everything that belongs to the Father flows through Jesus; everything that belongs to Jesus flows through the Spirit. What the Spirit is delivering to you, what He is causing you to fully know and comprehend, is directly from the Father; from the Father to the Son, from the Son to the Spirit, from the Spirit to you. The Father, living in you, is doing His work.

The Spirit Speaks Through You

Go back to the passage in John 14:10–11, where I asked you to place a mental marker. We looked far enough in the passage to see that Jesus told His listeners that He was speaking the Father's words and the Father, Who lived in Jesus, was doing His work. Then Jesus continued by saying, "'I tell you the truth, anyone who has faith in me will do what I have been doing. He will do even greater things than these, because I am going to the Father'" (John 14:12). Do you see? The work that the Father had been doing on earth through the physical vehicle of Jesus, He would continue to do when that physical vehicle was removed and replaced with the Spirit life of Jesus. The Father would from then on do His work through anyone in whom Jesus lives. This new work would be quantitatively greater because He would be doing it through many bodies, not just one. He would do not better works, but more works.

Jesus tells us that we will operate in the earth environment the same way He operated in the earth environment. The Father will speak through the Son, the Son will speak through the Spirit, the Spirit will speak through you. You will speak what you have heard from the Father. When you speak, it can be said of you, "That's her Father talking."

An Instructed Tongue

Isaiah 50:4 says:

> "The Sovereign Lord has given me an instructed tongue, to know the word that sustains the weary. He wakens me morning by morning, wakens my ear to listen like one being taught."

The Sovereign Lord wants to give you an "instructed tongue." He wants you to speak words taught you by the Spirit. (See 1 Cor. 2:13.) When you speak with an instructed tongue, what kind of power do your words have? They have the power to sustain the weary.

Words generated in my own wisdom can reach only as far as a person's intellect or feelings. They cannot reach to the core of a person—his spirit center; but words that are taught by the Spirit reach deep into the center and touch the spirit:

"Deep calls to deep" (Psalm 42:7). Spirit-generated words can touch the spirit because they are "expressing spiritual truths in spiritual words" (1 Cor. 2:13). These words are spiritual words because they were born of the Spirit. Everything that is born of the Spirit is spirit.

How do you learn the words that lift up the weary? "He wakens me morning by morning, wakens my ear to listen like one being taught" (Isa. 50:4). You learn by listening—listening carefully, attentively—like a student soaking up every word his mentor speaks. Respond to the Father's initiative. He wakens you morning after morning and unstops your spiritual ears.

The Father wants to speak His healing, encouraging, strengthening, eternal, life-giving words through your mouth. He wants to instruct your tongue. When He sends His word out through you, He has already given that word an assignment. The astonishing power of His Word will accomplish what He desires and purposes. (Read Isa. 55:10–11.)

As you live moment by moment in His power and presence, he will speak His present-tense word through you. "The lips of the righteous nourish many" (Prov. 10:21).

Appropriating the Power to Speak the Word

Let this prayer be yours:

Give my words wings, Lord.
May they alight gently on the branches of men's minds bending them to the winds of Your will.
May they fly high enough to touch the lofty, low enough to breathe the breath
Of sweet encouragement upon the downcast soul.

Give my words wings, Lord.
May they fly swift and far,
Winning the race with the words of the worldly wise, to the hearts of men.

Give my words wings, Lord. See them now nesting—down at
    Thy feet.
Silenced into ecstasy home at last.
                                        —Jill Briscoe[1]

Reflection Questions
1. What difference do you believe it would make in your
environment if you spoke with a tongue that had been
instructed by the Father?

2. Do you really believe that the very life of Jesus can flow
through you into your environment?

3. Have you discovered that the Father's words can do what
your words cannot? Do you continue to put faith in your
own words?

4. Will you commit yourself to listen to the Spirit Who lives
in you and learn from Him what to say and how to say it?

5. What changes do you need to make in your lifestyle or
attitudes to allow his life and power to flow through your
words?

Experience 2

Break the Scriptures down into phrases. Beside each phrase, write out your sense of what that phrase means. Add any Scripture references that shed new light on a thought. Write down or draw out any "verbal visuals." Add your thoughts or restate my thoughts so they match yours.
(John 8:26,28)

	My thoughts	Other Scriptures
He who sent me	*I am sent. I am on assignment. I am chosen and appointed. I have been summoned by name. My life has purpose.*	John 15:16
		Eph. 2:10
		Isa. 45:3
		Isa. 43:1
		John 20: 21
is reliable	*Is trustworthy; can be counted on; cannot lie because untruth is not in His nature; has no hidden agenda.*	Titus 1:2
		Rom. 3:4
		John 17:17
and what I have heard from him	*The truths He has caused me to understand; the things He has spoken to me and caused my spirit ears to hear*	Matt. 11:15
		1 Cor 2:9–10
		1 Cor. 4:1
		Prov. 2:6
I tell the world . . .	*I speak into my environment.*	Matt. 10:27
I do nothing on my own	*I rely on the life of Jesus transmitted to me by the Spirit.*	Col. 1:29
		2 Cor. 3:4–5
		2 Cor. 4:7
		Gal. 2:20

but	*In contrast to;* *instead of*	
speak	*Say only*	Prov. 16:23
just what	*the Father's*	Prov. 12:18
the Father	*life-giving*	Prov. 10:11
has taught me.	*words.*	

(John 14:24)

These words you hear	*The words* *being spoken* *with my voice;* *the word-sounds* *falling on my* *physical ears*	
are not my own;	*Did not originate* *in my flesh; are* *not worldly wise* *words; do not* *have the limitations* *of earthborn words.*	
they belong to the Father	*The Father owns* *them; they are* *His property;* *He is sending* *them out.*	Isa. 55:10–11
who sent me.	*The Father has* *assigned the words* *that He wants me* *to speak.*	

Restate the Scripture: *My trustworthy, truth-speaking Father has sent me into my environment to speak His message in every situation. He speaks His words to my spirit ears and I speak them into my world.*

Visual thoughts: *I imagine a TV news anchorperson with a listening device hidden in his ear. The producer in the control booth is reading him a breaking news story line by line. The anchor speaks exactly the words the producer is telling him to speak, but it appears to viewers that they are the anchor's own words. The producer is speaking through the mouth of the anchor. Similarly, God's words are flowing into my spirit ears, being processed in my understanding, and being spoken through my mouth.*

Experience 3

What questions do these passages answer? Go through the passages and state the question to which each phrase is an answer. Use my thoughts as a guide, but don't feel bound by them.

"'He who sent me is reliable, and what I have heard from him I tell the world' . . . 'I do nothing on my own but speak just what the Father has taught me'" (John 8:26,28).

"'These words you hear are not my own; they belong to the Father who sent me'" (John 14:24).

Q: Are you where you are because of random happenings?
A: No. God has sent me.

Q: Is the One Who sent you changeable and unreliable?
A: No. He is reliable.

Q: How do I know His thoughts?
A: He tells them to me; I have heard them from Him.

Q: What am I to do with what He teaches me?
A: He has sent me to speak His Words into my world.

Q: Should I do anything in my own strength?
A: No. I should act and speak by drawing on His Spirit in me.

Q: Instead of speaking on my own initiative, what should I speak?
A: Just exactly what the Father has taught me.

Q: Even when Spirit-born words are being articulated with my voice, are they my words?
A: No. Even though people in my world are hearing my voice, they are hearing the Father's words.

Q: Who is the owner of the Spirit-born words I speak?
A: They belong to the Father Who sent me.

Experience 4

Write out what you are hearing God say to you as you dig for the treasure in His Word. How is He addressing you? What term of endearment is He using? Write your own thoughts.

_____:

You are longing to hear Me speak and I am longing to speak. Don't let the fear of hearing Me incorrectly, or mistaking My voice for your imagination, stop you. Don't worry about your ability to hear. Trust My ability to speak. I'm initiating this interchange. We'll start out slowly while you learn the language of Spirit. I'll speak in your vocabulary. One step at a time. Here—take hold of My hand. Sit at My feet.

Leave it all to Me.

Experience 5

Write out what you want to say to God. Address Him lovingly and intimately. Add your own thoughts or restate this prayer to match your feelings.

_____:

You know the longing in me that is so deep I can't find the words to express it. You created that longing. I am like a parched land where there is no water. I can't soak up enough of You. I want to know You intimately. "Guide me in your truth and teach me" (Psalm 25:5). "I rejoice in your promise like one who finds great spoil" (Psalm 119:162). "The law from your mouth is more precious to me than thousands of pieces of silver and gold" (Psalm 119:72).

Let my mind and understanding be the tablet on which You write. I offer myself to You. Let me be the vehicle through which You do Your work in my world. Let Your words come from my mouth. Father, as I meditate on Your Word day and night, don't let Your words depart out of my mouth. Keep my mouth filled with Your words. I don't want to fill my mouth with any other words because then Your words won't be there.

Experience 6

Write out the promises God has made to you from His Word. Write the name(s) of those for whom you are harvesting each promise.

1. _____ *is/am on assignment from the Father.*
*Date*_____

2. *I will speak My Words to* _____ *in a way* _____
can understand.
*Date:*_____

3. _____ *can hear from God.*
*Date:*_____

Experience 7

Write out the faith statements that God has implanted in you as you have listened to Him. Make these the basis of your praise and worship.

✞ *God is reliable.*

✞ *God has placed me where I am. My life is not random.*

✞ *God is speaking to me and through me.*

✞ *I can let the Father do His work through me.*

✞ *The words God teaches me belong to Him and He will take responsibility for them.*

Worship with abandon in your secret sanctuary!

¹From *Wings* by Jill Briscoe. Used by permission.

THE APPOINTED WAY

Experience 1

"Who, then, is the man that fears the Lord? He will instruct him in the way chosen for him. He will spend his days in prosperity, and his descendants will inherit the land. The Lord confides in those who fear him; he makes his covenant known to them" (*Psalm 25:12–14*). (*Focal passage: Psalm 25:8–14*)

"Show me a person who fears the Lord. I want to see what such a person would be like," David says in Psalm 25:12. Like David, I want to see in some tangible form a person who is what I want to be—a person who fears the Lord. To fear the Lord means to deeply reverence the Lord. How is deep reverence for the Lord lived out? What does it look like when it is translated from desiring and willing into doing? What does a person who fears the Lord look like? He looks like Jesus.

The Father sent the Son to show how a person who reverences the Lord lives. Jesus obeyed every one of the Father's words while He lived on the earth. He showed us that uncompromising obedience to the Father's voice is the way to show reverence to the Lord.

Sometimes the best way to understand a concept is to look at its opposite. What is the opposite of reverence? The flip side of reverence is contempt. Observe how God has defined contempt. In Numbers 14, we read the story of the Israelites' refusal to follow God into the Promised Land. They chose to fear the inhabitants of the land rather than to reverence God.

They had unshakable faith in the inhabitants' ability to defeat them, and no faith in God's ability to deliver them the victory. God called this misplaced faith contempt. He said to Moses, "'How long will these people treat me with contempt? How long will they refuse to believe in me?'" (Num. 14:11). When we refuse to trust God and follow His direction, and instead ascribe power to earthly circumstances, we are treating God with contempt. When we focus our faith on God and recognize that earthly circumstances are only the stage for the display of His power, we are reverencing Him.

Fear of the Lord Produces Joy

Jesus is our pattern for what fearing the Lord looks like. The trait that seemed to define Jesus' life was joy. Have you noticed how often Jesus talked about His joy? He prayed for His followers that "'they may have the full measure of my joy within them'" (John 17:13). He said to His disciples, after teaching them that His life would flow through them, "'I have told you this so that my joy may be in you and that your joy may be complete'" (John 15:11). Jesus is so often portrayed as solemn, burdened, and stoic that we have lost the sense of His joy. Yet the Scripture paints Him as joyful. Children loved to be around Him. People were attracted to Him, followed Him, wanted to be in His presence. His accusers called Him a friend of sinners. I can't imagine sinners, or nonreligious people, counting someone as friend who was dour and moody and depressed. I think that in His physical form He must have been delightful and witty and magnetic. I know that He is so in His Spirit form.

One of the most obvious characteristics of a person who fears the Lord, then, is joy. Jesus modeled joy during His physical life and imparts joy through His Spirit life. What was the spark for this joy?

Joy Sparked By Purposeful Living

In our focus passage, after David asks, "Who, then, is the man that fears the Lord?" he goes on to explain why he wants to know. The one who fears the Lord is the person who will know "the way chosen for him." That person will walk in the way directed by the Father—the way the Father laid out for him before time began. "We are God's workmanship, created in Christ Jesus to do good works, which God prepared in advance for us to do" (Eph. 2:10).

The Creator has placed into humans a craving for purpose and direction. This craving is meant to lead each person to the One Who created him with a specific purpose in mind. A sense of purpose gives meaning to life. It creates a joyful, expectant outlook. The keener the sense of calling or purpose, the more satisfied one feels. Your purpose, my purpose, was assigned to us before we were born on Planet Earth. When we were nothing but a plan of God, our purpose was already assigned. The timing of your birth, the location of your home, the family into which God placed you, the experiences God has allowed and the experiences He has engineered—all have to do with a preassigned purpose. God put you on the earth when and where you could accomplish your purpose and find the way chosen for you. "'Before I formed you in the womb I knew you, before you were born I set you apart'" (Jer. 1:5). "Your eyes saw my unformed body. All the days ordained for me were written in your book before one of them came to be" (Psalm 139:16).

A person does not have to live his or her purpose. A person may choose not to live God's design for his life. God does not coerce a person into living purposefully and with meaning, but He invites it; He makes it possible.

A sense of destiny, a reason for being, a feeling of value—all come from discovering purpose. A strong sense of purpose produces joy. Even the hard times and the confusing circumstances and the seeming setbacks will be fused into an understanding of destiny. The person who lives with a focused purpose will see life as something like a jigsaw puzzle, each piece fitting into a pattern to produce the whole. If you were to look at a single piece of a jigsaw puzzle, it would seem meaningless and random. Yet when you place it in its assigned position, it becomes an integral part of the picture. When one piece of the puzzle is missing, the picture is not whole. When you look at the circumstances of your life as if each could stand alone, and as if each situation should make sense on its own, you will never see the Big Picture. Only when you view each happening as a significant piece of a whole, will you begin to see life as integrated and meaningful. As God works in your life, He is keeping His eye on the Big Picture. He is directing you in the way chosen for you. Rejoice!

Listen to your Father. Hear Him as He assures you: "'I am the Lord your God, who teaches you what is best for you, who directs you in the way you should go'" (Isa. 48:17). Jesus, operating in the earth environment, knew this. His sense of purpose and destiny was strong. "'The Son of Man came to seek and to save what was lost'" (Luke 19:10).

His sense of purpose gave Him wisdom in making decisions. When the crowds were imploring Him to stay with them, Jesus said, "'I must preach the good news of the kingdom of God to the other towns also, because that is why I was sent'" (Luke 4:43).

His sense of purpose enabled Him to serve instead of demanding to be served. "Jesus knew that the Father had put all things under his power, and that he had come from God and was returning to God; so he got up from the meal, took off his outer clothing, and wrapped a towel around his waist. . . . He . . . began to wash his disciples' feet" (John 13:3–5).

His sense of purpose sustained Him through the agonizing days of rejection, humiliation, torture, and death. "'Now my heart is troubled, and what shall I say? "Father, save me from this hour?" No, it was for this very reason I came to this hour. Father, glorify yourself'" (John 12:27–28).

Jesus walked in the way chosen for Him, and He lived joyfully. He showed us what it would look like to fear the Lord. In the continual search for meaning and direction, this truth emerges: When we find His way, we find our way.

His Way: Prosperity

David writes that the one who fears the Lord, who walks in the chosen way, will "spend his days in prosperity." The word *prosperity* means being secure or well-supplied. When we walk in our preassigned purpose, we will always have the success that God preassigned. Success manifests itself differently according to differing assignments. Only God can define your success, but you will recognize it and embrace it. When you are walking in His path, "in all things at all times, having all that you need, you will abound in every good work. . . . Now he who supplies seed to the sower and bread for food will also supply and increase your store of seed and will enlarge the harvest of your righteousness" (2 Cor. 9:8–10).

The prosperity that God ordains for you will be passed down through generations to come. "His descendants will inherit the land." The Old Covenant picture of land is translated in New Covenant as spiritual abundance and rest. (See Heb. 4.) You will leave a legacy of faith and spiritual riches to your descendants.

God Tells His Secrets

He "takes the upright into his confidence" (Prov. 3:32). "The Lord confides in those who fear him" (Psalm 25:14). What does He confide? Our focus passage says He "makes known his covenant." He interprets His covenant to His friends so that they understand what it means. The covenant in which you and I live is a covenant of fulfillment. When we understand the covenant, we experience the promises fulfilled. Only God fully understands the covenant, and He explains it to His intimate friends.

Do you want the Father to whisper His confidences to you? Reverence Him. Don't treat Him with contempt by ignoring His word to you. Put your confidence in Him and He will confide in you.

Reflection Questions

1. Are you wandering aimlessly through life waiting for the happening that will change everything or do you have a strong sense of God's purpose in your life?

2. Have you discovered the way chosen for you?

3. Are you reverencing the Lord, or treating Him with contempt?

4. What circumstances in your life are causing you to fear?

5. Ask the Spirit how to redefine those circumstances and refocus your faith. What is He saying?

6. Do you have joy in your life? If not, ask the Spirit what is robbing you of the joy. If so, ask the Spirit to help you define, in words or pictures, the source of your joy.

Experience 2

Break the Scripture down into phrases. Beside each phrase, write out your interpretation of that phrase. Write down other Scripture references that shed more light on each thought. Write out or sketch out any visual language. Use my thoughts only as a guide.

(Psalm 25:12–14)	My thoughts	Other Scriptures
Who, then, is the man	*Show me a person*	
that fears the Lord?	*Who lives in uncompromising obedience to the Lord.*	
He will instruct him	*As I fear the Lord, He will give me instructions; He will show me the path to walk.*	Psalm 25:4–5 Psalm 119:35 Psalm 32:8
in the way chosen for him.	*God has already marked out a way for me to walk; He has a purpose for me.*	Psalm 138:8
He will spend his days	*I will live each day*	
in prosperity,	*fully supplied; as I live out my purpose, God will provide everything I need. Since my purpose is really His purpose, He will be providing the resources for His purpose when He meets my needs.*	

and his descendants	*My reverence for God will flow to my descendants, either physical or spiritual descendants.*	Prov. 14:26
will inherit the land.	*My descendants will inherit the spiritual promised land; they will have easier access to the land; they must choose for themselves to put down roots and make it home, but it will be theirs to possess.*	Psalm 102:28 Isa. 54:13 Isa. 44:3–5 Isa. 59:21
The Lord confides in	*The Lord tells His secrets to*	1 Cor. 4:1–2
those who fear him;	*those who obey and trust Him; me.*	
he makes his covenant known	*He explains His covenant; He discloses the power of covenant; He speaks the promises*	
to them.	*to me.*	

Restate the Scripture: *The more I walk in uncompromising obedience to the Lord's voice, the deeper will be my sense of purpose and destiny. As I walk in the way God has chosen for me, I will see the fulfillment of all His covenant promises in my life. I will be fully supplied and secure. I will grow in intimacy with the Lord and will pass spiritual prosperity on to my descendants.*

Visual thoughts: *I imagine a walking trail. It has one starting point and one ending point, but the trail has various twists and turns along the way. The trail is marked with arrows of different colors, so that if I want to walk four miles, I should follow the red arrows; if I want to walk three miles, I should follow the green arrows. Each walker is walking a different version of the same path.*

On my life path, my starting point is Jesus and my ending point is heaven. If I am careful to observe, I will be able to follow the path God has chosen and marked out for me.

Experience 3

What questions does this passage answer? Go through the passage and ask the questions to which you find answers.

"Who, then, is the man that fears the Lord? He will instruct him in the way chosen for him. He will spend his days in prosperity, and his descendants will inherit the land. The Lord confides in those who fear him; he makes his covenant known to them" (Psalm 25:12–14).

Q: Who will receive instruction from the Lord?
A: The one who fears Him.

Q: What instructions will the Lord give this person?
A: The way chosen for him.

Q: Do I choose or create my own way, my own destiny?
A: No. It is chosen for me.

Q: Who chose my way?
A: God.

Q: Once I am on my way, am I on my own?
A: No. God is fully supplying me and giving me security.

Q: Will I ever go one day without God's supply?
A: No. I will spend my days in prosperity.

Q: Can I have an impact on the lives of my descendants?
A: Yes. My fear of the Lord will transfer the deed to the land to my descendants.

Q: In whom does the Lord confide?
A: Me.

Q: What does He confide?
A: He explains the covenant.

Experience 4

Write out what you are sensing God is saying to you. This week, I will write out some of my thoughts. You write out your own. How do you hear God addressing you?

_____:

I formed you exactly how I needed you to be to fulfill My purpose. I have already marked out a path for you to follow. Along that path you will find your longings fulfilled; you will find your needs met. Along that path, you will find yourself in Me. I have placed all of your provision along your path. You will not find them along anyone else's path. They are waiting for you on the path marked "_____'s Way."

(Put your name.)

As you walk your path, you will encounter the good deeds I have assigned you to do. I assigned them before you existed. Don't try to do anyone else's deeds. They are not assigned for you. You have to fix your eyes on Me and keep your ears open toward Me so that I can lead you step-by-step along your path. Every time you come to a decision, I'll be there saying, "This is the way. Walk in it."

I need for you to be completely abandoned to Me. I need to have access to all of you. I need your fixed attention at all times. This is how you reverence Me. Your reverence opens the way for Me to confide in you and to disclose your purpose and the meaning of your life. Follow Me. I will fill you with joy.

Experience 5

Write out your heartfelt, honest response to the Father. Today I will write out my thoughts. Add your own. How will you address Him?

_____:

Thank You, thank You, thank You! You have filled my life with such a deep sense of purpose. I can't imagine living without meaning. You need me. I know that You only need me because You have chosen to need me, but still You need me to fulfill my purpose so that You can fulfill Your purpose. Every day of my life is an adventure as I walk deeper into Your purpose for me.

Remember when I first sensed a personal destiny? Remember how cautiously I started down my path? The way seemed so dark and unknowable, but You kept encouraging me to take baby steps. Sometimes I stumbled over obstacles I didn't see. Sometimes I skinned a knee. But You always picked me up and moved me on. The farther I traveled, the more clear the path became. More often than not, I now see the obstacles before I trip over them. The journey is shaping me. I am becoming stronger and bolder as I travel. I still have a long way to go, but now sometimes I can even pick up the pace for a while. I love the way You have chosen for me!

Teach me how to fear You and reverence You and worship You more. When I look away, draw me back. When I hesitate, push me forward. When I wander, find me. Fill me with love for You. Take me into Your confidence. Continue to instruct me in the way You have chosen for me.

Experience 6

What promises has God made to you from His Word? Write them down. Beside each, write the person(s) for whom you prayed this promise and the date you prayed it. (The name you write may be yours.)

This week I will write some of my own thoughts. Add your own. Change these to make them personal and specific to your life.

1. God will personally instruct _____ *and teach* _____ *how to walk out his or her destiny.*
Date _____

2. God has already marked out a path for _____.
He has placed along _____ *'s path the fulfill-ment of all the promises He has made.*
Date _____

3. _____ *will spend* _____ *'s days fully supplied and secure.*
Date _____

4. _____ *'s descendants will inherit the land.*
Date _____

5. God will confide in _____ .
Date _____

6. _____ *will see God's covenant promises operative in* _____ *'s life.*
Date _____

Experience 7

Write out faith statements that have taken shape as you have inquired of the Spirit this week. Let these be the basis of your time of extended praise and worship.

✞ *God will instruct me.*

✞ *God has created me for a specific purpose.*

✞ *God has marked my way. He will show it to me.*

✞ *God will provide for my every need.*

✞ *God will work in the lives of my descendants because of my reverence for Him.*

✞ *The Lord will confide in me.*

Worship with abandon in your secret sanctuary!

THE TRIUMPHAL MARCH

Experience 1

"Thanks be to God, who always leads us in triumphal procession in Christ and through us spreads everywhere the fragrance of the knowledge of him. For we are to God the aroma of Christ among those who are being saved and those who are perishing. To the one we are the smell of death; to the other, the fragrance of life" *(2 Cor. 2:14–16).*

"Thanks be to God, who always leads us in triumphal procession in Christ," Paul says. Paul is drawing on an image from the Roman culture. He creates a mental picture of a triumphal procession in which a triumphant Roman general is celebrated for his victorious campaign. The conquering general is preceded into the city by the captives taken in war and is followed by his triumphant troops. As the conquering troops parade through the city, they shout "Triumph!"

Triumphal Procession in Christ

We live in one continual triumphal march that began at the cross and goes on endlessly into eternity. The triumphal procession in which we march is headed by Jesus, the Conqueror. "And having disarmed the powers and authorities, he made a public spectacle of them, triumphing over them by the cross" (Col. 2:15). Our enemies, whom the Scriptures

65

makes clear are the powers, principalities, and authorities of Satan's realm, are the army over whom Jesus has triumphed. (Read Eph. 6:12.) The battleground on which the victory has been won is the cross of Jesus. The conquering army is made up of believers—you and me. We are to be marching through life with the shout of "Triumph!" on our lips, spreading everywhere the fragrance of the knowledge of Him.

The Power of Aroma

Through His army, God is spreading the fragrance of Jesus everywhere. Of all the physical senses, the sense of smell is the strongest. Aromas are imprinted on the memory. You remember everything you have ever smelled and the memory of it is activated when you smell the aroma again. An aroma will stir up a memory and all the emotions attached to it. Perhaps when you smell cinnamon, you are transported in your memory to your grandmother's kitchen and the aroma of cinnamon creates in you a sense of being warm and safe and loved.

Smell, when it is pleasant, draws you to its source. It awakens a desire in you to possess the source. When you walk into a grocery store and smell freshly baked bread, what happens? You begin to desire freshly baked bread. Smell stirs up something called sensory integration. All of your senses become involved in the desiring. You imagine how freshly baked bread looks, feels, and tastes. Finally, you purchase freshly baked bread. How interesting, then, that the Creator, Who created the senses, should choose the picture of aroma to teach us how Christ is made known to the world.

Included in the Roman triumphal procession were the priests of Jupiter swinging censers filled with burning incense. The streets and temple were decorated with fragrant garlands. Aroma was an important feature of the triumphal procession. Paul says that the aroma of Jesus is central to our victory march. To some, he says, it is the smell of death; to others, the smell of life. When the Roman procession reached its destination, the temple of Jupiter, the captives were led off to their execution. The aroma of the procession was a smell that denoted victory for the triumphant and death for the defeated. The same smell held differing meanings, depending upon one's position in the procession.

My dad grew up on a farm in Missouri. I remember as a child when we would visit a farm, my nose would be assaulted with the horrible smells of animals and hay and farm things. As I was thinking, What a terrible smell! my dad would say, "I just love these smells!" I always wondered whether we were smelling the same aroma, or if grown-ups could smell things children could not.

The very same aroma was a sweet savor to my dad and an awful stench to me. The same smell had different emotional associations for each of us and those associations determined its impact. Paul tells us that the aroma of Christ is wafting through the world, both to those who are in the process of being saved and to those who are in the process of dying eternally. To one it is the smell of life, to the other it is the stench of death. It attracts the one and repels the other. His children call out, "Your name is like perfume poured out" (Song of Songs 1:3). Among His enemies, His name is reviled and ridiculed and defamed. Same aroma, different reactions.

Only Jesus Smells Like Jesus

An aroma identifies its source. A rose, for example, emits an aroma that you will immediately identify as a rose. "I smell a rose," you will say. A rose may have many different names as it is translated into different languages, but the smell identifies it as a rose. "A rose by any other name would smell as sweet," Shakespeare wrote.

The aroma of Christ comes from the life of Christ. The fragrance of Christ will not be produced by good works, or moral behavior, or by answering correctly, or by following the rules. Only Jesus smells like Jesus.

Paul says that the aroma of Christ is introduced into the world through you and me: "who . . . through us spreads everywhere the fragrance of the knowledge of him." We are the censers that hold the sweet-smelling incense. Jesus' life is operating on earth in and through us. He lives in us and is expressed through us. As His life comes through us, the world can breathe in His aroma.

A Yielded Life: A Sweet-Smelling Aroma

"We are the fragrance of Christ to God," says Paul. A sweet-smelling fragrance rose to God from the burnt sacrifices of the ceremonial system, which pictured spiritual reality in a tangible form. This aroma gave Him pleasure. "This is the regular burnt offering instituted at Mount Sinai as a pleasing aroma, an offering made to the Lord by fire" (Num. 28:6).

Paul tells us in Romans 12:1 that the offering we are to present is our own bodies. He says, "Offer your bodies as living sacrifices, holy and pleasing to God—which is your spiritual act of worship" (Rom. 12:1). He uses the phrase, "pleasing to God." This phrase echoes the Old Covenant phrase used to describe burnt offerings. Burnt offerings always produced a pleasing aroma to the Lord. What is Paul describing? How do you and I become the pleasing aroma of Christ to God? We offer our bodies, our physical structure, to God to be instruments through which He acts out His will. His response is pictured in Leviticus 9:24: "Fire came out from the presence of the Lord and consumed the burnt offering and the fat portions on the altar." God Himself sends the Spirit Who appears in our lives as fire. He proceeds to burn away everything in us that is temporal and to purify everything in us that is of eternal significance.

"The fire on the altar must be kept burning; it must not go out" (Lev. 6:13). We are not to "quench the Spirit," which means we are not to put out the Spirit's fire. We perform our priestly service of offering worship by yielding our lives to Him. Then we are a pleasing aroma to the Lord; then He can use us to spread the fragrance.

"And live a life of love, just as Christ loved us and gave himself up for us as a fragrant offering and sacrifice to God" (Eph. 5:2).

Reflection Questions

1. Do you feel that you are marching in Jesus' triumphal procession? If not, specifically what is making you feel defeated?

2. If you are feeling defeated, is your feeling the truth?

3. Write down the lie you are believing. Write down the truth that contradicts it. Would you be willing to line yourself up with the truth and disregard the lie?

4. Have you offered yourself as a living sacrifice to God? If not, would you do so now?

5. If you have presented yourself a living sacrifice, have you been trying to ignite the fire on the altar yourself? Would you now ask God to send fire from His presence and keep it burning continually?

Experience 2

Beside each phrase, write out your own sense of what that phrase has come to mean. Write out any other corresponding Scripture references that come to mind. Describe or sketch any visual ideas that the words ignite.

This week I have divided the phrases and included some Scripture references. You do the rest.

(2 Cor. 2:14–16)	My thoughts	Other Scriptures
Thanks be to God,		
who always leads us		Ex. 15:13 Isa. 42:16
in triumphal procession		Rom. 8:35–39 1 John 5:4–5 Josh. 5:1
in Christ		John 16:33
and through us		2 Cor. 5:20
spreads everywhere		Prov. 15:7

the fragrance of the   Isa. 11:9
knowledge of him.

For we are to God
the aroma of Christ

among those who are
being saved

and those who are perishing.

To the one we are the smell   John 17:14–16
of death;   John 15:18–19

to the other, the fragrance   John 1:4
of life.

Restate the Scripture:

Visual thoughts:

Experience 3

What questions does this Scripture answer? This week I will write out some questions. You supply the answers.

"Thanks be to God, who always leads us in triumphal procession in Christ and through us spreads everywhere the fragrance of the knowledge of him. For we are to God the aroma of Christ among those who are being saved and those who are perishing. To the one we are the smell of death; to the other, the fragrance of life" (2 Cor. 2:14–16).

Q: Will Jesus ever lead me in defeat?

Q: Is my victory to be kept secret?

Q: Is my triumph anywhere except in Christ?

Q: How does God spread the knowledge of Christ?

Q: Where does God spread the knowledge of Christ?

Q: Does the aroma of Christ have the same effect on everyone? What makes the difference?

Experience 4

What is the Father saying to you?

Experience 5

What is your response to the Father?

Experience 6

What promises has God made to you from His Word? Write them down. Beside each, write the name(s) of the person(s) for whom you prayed this promise and the date you prayed.

Experience 7

Write out faith statements for your life. Let these be the basis of your praise and worship.

Worship with abandon in your secret sanctuary!

MY ROCK AND MY SALVATION

Experience 1

"Find rest, O my soul, in God alone; my hope comes from him. He alone is my rock and my salvation; he is my fortress, I will not be shaken. My salvation and my honor depend on God; he is my mighty rock, my refuge. Trust in him at all times, O people; pour out your hearts to him, for God is our refuge" (Psalm 62:5–8). (Focal passage: Psalm 62:1–8)

Only in God will my inner person find rest. God is the resting place for His children. Jesus' invitation is: "'Come to me, all you who are weary and burdened, and I will give you rest. Take my yoke upon you and learn from me, for I am gentle and humble in heart, and you will find rest for your souls. For my yoke is easy and my burden is light'" (Matt. 11:28–30).

God is not the burden giver. He is the burden bearer. If you are carrying a soul burden, God wants to lift it from you. He wants you to find rest and relief from burdens you were never meant to carry. He is your soul's home. Anywhere but in Him you are an outsider. You will find soul rest only in God. "He restores my soul" (Psalm 23:3).

Your Hope Comes from God

God is the only source of everything your soul hopes and longs for. The hope that God offers is not like hope the world offers. Earth hope is wishful thinking. God hope is confident, sure expectation. The word *hope* literally means "a cord." It comes from a primary root word meaning "entwining."

Picture the hope God offers you like this: You have fallen into a deep ravine. As you look around, you see no means of escape. The ravine is so deep that no one will hear you if you cry for help. The walls are so steep and so treacherous that climbing is out of the question. You are in a hopeless situation from which you cannot rescue yourself.

Suddenly you look up and see a person at the top of the ravine. What kind of hope does that inspire in you? It can only inspire wishful thinking. Your hope is shadowy and insubstantial: "If only there was some way for that person to reach me, I would be saved."

You notice that the person has a rope. Your hope now has a little more substance: "If that rope is long enough to reach me and strong enough to hold me, I could be saved."

The rescuer throws down the rope. It is long enough. It is strong enough. You wrap it securely around your waist and grab hold of it with your hands. Your hope has a more solid basis. "If that person is strong enough to pull me up, I will be saved."

You recognize the rescuer. He is the strongest person who has ever lived. His exploits are legendary. Pulling your weight won't even tax his strength. This will be easy for him. Your hope becomes confidence. "I will be saved."

Now you have God hope. Anxiety is gone. As long as you cling to that rope, you are being pulled out of the ravine by the strongest person who ever lived. At times, the pace may be slow. At times, the path may be difficult, but you are bound to your rescuer by a strong rope, which is entwined around you. Your hope comes from him.

Isn't that a wonderful picture? You are bound to God by a cord called hope. Because of Who He is, you have the confident expectation that He will save you from any situation.

God Is Your Rock and Your Salvation

He alone is your rock. He alone is solid ground for your feet. He alone is sure and immovable. "They trust God not at all who trust him not alone. He that stands with one foot on a rock, and another foot upon a quicksand, will sink and perish, as certainly as he that standeth with both feet upon a quicksand."[1]

God Is Your Fortress

He alone is your fortress. He alone is the protector from all your enemies. He is your security and your safety. He is your hiding place from danger. "You are my hiding place; you will protect me from trouble and surround me with songs of deliverance" (Psalm 32:7).

When I was a little girl, when darkness fell, I was certain that terrible monsters were lurking in my room, just waiting to eat me up. As my fear grew, I would finally be motivated to make the mad dash from my monster-infested room to my parents' room. I would jump into their bed right between them. Here I felt perfectly safe. Here I was fearless. I still thought the monsters were around. I just knew that they couldn't get to me in my safe position between my parents. When I was safely in my parents' bed, I could sleep peacefully in spite of the monsters. I knew that no monsters could get past them. They were my fortress.

Hidden in Him, surrounded by Him, protected by Him you will never be dislodged from your firm footing. He is "an impregnable castle" (Psalm 62:2 *The Message*).

Your Salvation and Your Honor Come from God

Your salvation, your freedom from any oppressive or repressive circumstances in life, depends on Him.

Your honor comes from Him. The word *honor* means "weight" in the context of determining and assigning value. The weightier, the more valuable. It means your essence, the substance of who you are, the eternal weightiness of your soul. Your extreme value depends on, or comes from, Him alone.

We have a colloquial phrase that means "to impart one's own value to another." The phrase is *throw your weight behind* another. A person who has little stature of his own gains stature when someone important and powerful endorses him. If the powerful individual is willing to link his reputation with that of the person of lesser stature and make his resources available for that person's use, the man is now a man to be reckoned with. Someone powerful has thrown his weight behind the person—has imparted his value to another. God has thrown His weight behind you. Your honor comes from Him. You are someone to be reckoned with.

God Is Your Mighty Rock and Your Refuge

He is your mighty rock. In desert life, a large rock was highly valued because it provided shade from the scorching sun as well as protection from the ever-blowing winds. In the shade provided by a mighty rock, plant life could grow and flourish. You live in His protecting shadow where you can flourish. He is your mighty rock, your refuge. He blocks the fierce elements that would deplete your strength and uproot you. In His shadow, your life can become "like a well-watered garden" (Isa. 58:11).

You can trust in Him at all times. Good times, bad times, frightening times, grieving times, rejoicing times, difficult times, faith-stretching times, lonely times, longing times . . . trust in Him at all times. He is trustworthy and reliable in all situations. He is your rock.

Pour Out Your Heart

You can pour out your heart to Him. When your heart is full of grief and doubt and fear and uncertainty, pour it out to Him. "Pour out your heart like water in the presence of the Lord" (Lam. 2:19). What happens when you pour out water? It evaporates. When you pour out your pain honestly before your loving, trustworthy, honorable, dependable Father, it begins to evaporate. Then your heart can be filled with "new wine," the wine of the Holy Spirit. We empty ourselves of our negative emotions and find healing and restoration in His presence. In Him alone will your soul find rest.

Reflection Questions

1. Does the word *secure* define you?

2. Why or why not?

3. From what do you need to be hidden? Name the "monsters" in your life from which you need protection and safety.

4. Before today, where have you sought safety and security?

5. What are you hoping and longing for?

6. What situation(s) looks hopeless to you? From what does there seem to be no rescue?

7. Is He the source of your hope, or are you putting your hope in something or someone else? Answer this question specifically for each hope or longing you listed in question 5.

8. Which description of God in this passage was most comforting and most encouraging to you?
❏ My rock
❏ My salvation
❏ My fortress
❏ My mighty rock
❏ My refuge

9. Why?

Experience 2

Examine the Scripture passage phrase by phrase and then write your sense of what that phrase means. As you reflect on each phrase, write down other Scriptures that come to mind. Describe any visual thoughts.

(Psalm 62:5–8)
Find rest, O my soul,

in God alone;

my hope comes from him.

He alone is my rock

and my salvation;

he is my fortress,

I will not be shaken.

My salvation and my
honor depend on God;

he is my mighty rock,

my refuge.

Trust in him at all times,
O people;

pour out your hearts to him,

for God is our refuge.

Restate the Scripture:

Visual thoughts:

Experience 3

What questions does this passage answer?

"Find rest, O my soul, in God alone; my hope comes from him. He alone is my rock and my salvation; he is my fortress, I will not be shaken. My salvation and my honor depend on God; he is my mighty rock, my refuge. Trust in him at all times, O people; pour out your hearts to him, for God is our refuge" (Psalm 62:5–8).

Experience 4

What is God saying to you? How is He addressing you?

Experience 5

What is your honest, heartfelt response to God? Write it out.
How will you address Him?

Experience 6

What promises has God made to you from His Word? Write them down. Beside each, write the name(s) of the person(s) for whom you have prayed this promise and the date you prayed.

Be specific about how these promises apply. For example, instead of writing *I will keep you safe,* write *God will keep me safe from . . .* and then name specific things from which you, or someone else, need safety. Instead of writing *I will not allow you to be shaken,* write *God will not allow me (or someone you are praying for) to be shaken by . . .* and then name a specific situation in which you need stability.

Experience 7

Write faith statements that God has made real to you in the process of contemplating His Word this week. Make them specific to your life or the lives of those for whom you are praying. Listen to the Spirit. Let these be the basis for your morning of honest praise and worship.

Worship with abandon!

[1]Charles H. Spurgeon, *The Treasury of David,* vol. 2 (McLean, VA: Macdonald Publishing Co., n.d.).

PRESS ON TOWARD THE GOAL

"I press on to take hold of that for which Christ Jesus took hold of me. . . . Forgetting what is behind and straining toward what is ahead, I press on toward the goal to win the prize for which God has called me heavenward in Christ Jesus" (Phil. 3:12–14). (Focal passage: Phil. 3:12–21)

Single-minded concentration; clear focus; directed vision; a runner racing for the finish line, distractions blocked out, hard-won goal in view: this is how Paul describes the faith journey.

"Press on," the Spirit tells us. The expression means "to pursue with earnestness and diligence in order to obtain." Don't settle for anything less than the goal. Don't compromise your vision. Don't let the distractions of the world slow your single-minded pursuit. Don't let circumstances or worries trip you up. Press on.

Keep Your Eyes on the Prize

What is this goal toward which the Spirit prods us? Paul puts it in these words: "to take hold of that for which Christ Jesus took hold of me." We see here a dichotomy. Two thoughts seem to be mutually exclusive. I would paraphrase this statement like this: "I am pursuing the thing that has already caught me." Jesus pursued Paul, as He does you and me, and

He caught him. Jesus entered into relationship with Paul for a purpose. He appointed Paul to take the message to the Gentile world. He had been preparing Paul throughout his whole life, even though Paul did not know Jesus as Messiah until he was a grown man. In the same way, Jesus has called you and me and appointed us to specific tasks even before we knew Him. Jesus wants you to take hold of the purpose for which He has taken hold of you.

Jesus took hold of Paul with the goal of conforming Paul into His own image. His purpose for Paul was that Paul become a vessel through which Jesus would live. From the beginning, Jesus planned that Paul would learn to empty himself of Paul and be filled with Jesus. From the outset, Jesus' intent was that Paul would see that his own successes were nothing but rubbish—were less than nothing—when compared to the surpassing worth of his new goal: knowing Jesus intimately.

He has sought you out. You long for Him because He longs for you. You love Him because He first loved you. You press on toward Him because He is drawing you. What feels like initiative is really a response. You yearn for what He is offering. His invitation has awakened your desire.

Leaving the Past Behind

"Forgetting what is behind and straining toward what is ahead, I press on." Look carefully at what the Spirit is teaching us. Stop and read Philippians 3:2–14 so that you can put these words into their proper setting and see the truth clearly.

The way to move forward is to be disentangled from your past. The Word says to forget what is behind. The word translated "forget" means to neglect. Don't nourish the past; don't give any attention to your past no matter how loudly it demands it.

Now look carefully at Paul's description of the past he is forgetting.

"If anyone else thinks he has reasons to put confidence in the flesh, I have more: circumcised on the eighth day, of the people of Israel, of the tribe of Benjamin, a Hebrew of Hebrews; in regard to the law, a Pharisee; as for zeal, persecuting the church; as for legalistic righteousness, faultless" (Phil. 2:5–6).

Paul is leaving behind a past filled with success, honor, and religion. He had a past to be proud of. His emphasis here is not leaving behind your failures, but leaving behind your successes. He is forgetting about and neglecting the things he once thought would make him righteous and fill his inward craving. He is leaving behind the behaviors that had worked in his flesh-driven life. Before Jesus, Paul had learned methods for getting his personal needs met.

You and I are like Paul. We have practiced and perfected behaviors that temporarily get our needs met. Do you recognize yours? Some, like Paul, drive themselves to be the best of the best because then they receive the love and approval they need. Some people have learned that complaining will get them attention that temporarily feels like love. Some people have practiced the technique of being a doormat and have learned that it seems to earn them the approval they crave. Some people try to get their need for love and approval met by being overbearing and controlling. Others put forth a facade of external religious rituals. The list of ingenious human behaviors has no end. The problem with these techniques is that they are only fleeting fixes; they have to be repeated over and over and over—just like the sacrificial system. We all have them. They are behavior patterns we have fixed in our lives through repetition. They seem normal and rational to us.

Paul says that if you and I want to seize with both hands the purpose for which Jesus has seized us, we have to leave behind every flesh-born pattern of behavior that we have relied on to attract love and make us feel valued. Is this harder for you than leaving behind past failures and sins? It is for me. God is calling us to stop using our tried-and-true approval-getting methods and have faith only in Him. I don't have to trust in my own ability to earn approval. I can trust His promise that He fully approves of me and accepts me based on the life of Jesus in me. I can relax in His power working in me to produce behavior that will be productive.

Pursue Righteousness

God tells us to pursue and strive for righteousness. However, He tells us to pursue it by the correct method. Otherwise, you are wasting energy and producing nothing. Don't box the air, don't run in place, don't waste energy. Paul writes in Romans 9:30–32, "What then shall we say? That the Gentiles, who did not pursue righteousness, have obtained it, a righteousness that is by faith; but Israel, who pursued the law of righteousness, has not attained to it? Why not? Because they pursued it not by faith but as if it were by works. They stumbled over the 'stumbling stone.'"

God said from the beginning that the Messiah would be a stumbling stone to some. He would actually cause some to stumble. Why? Because the Way to righteousness is so foreign to flesh thinking that many will not recognize Him. He is the cornerstone, the foundation of everything, for some; but He is a stumbling stone to others. The person who is banking on his or her ability to please God will stumble over the cornerstone. It is more sensible to our human wisdom that we should pursue righteousness as if it were by works. But God says that pursuing righteousness by our own methods will guarantee failure to obtain it.

The Righteousness That Comes from God

Define righteousness as "rightness." Righteousness is the state of being aligned with your eternal purpose—a dwelling place for the living God. When you are what you were created to be, you no longer have the nagging sense that "something's

not right." Instead, you have the deep-down sense of rightness. It doesn't mean that your actions and attitudes have
become perfect, but that you are on the right path toward the
right goal with the right resources at your disposal. You feel at
home.

Rightness comes from God and faith in Christ is what
brings it into your life. You will not find that sense of rightness in flesh-born pursuits. You will find it only in absolute
surrender to the Life within you, giving you freely the rightness you have been trying to earn. "'Why spend money on
what is not bread, and your labor on what does not satisfy?
Listen, listen to me, and eat what is good, and your soul will
delight in the richest of fare'" (Isa. 55:2). Stop working for
what is already yours. Let Him satisfy that hunger that won't
be satisfied, that thirst that won't be quenched.

Your only goal, your single-minded purpose, is to forget
the old patterns of depending on flesh energy and let God
flow in Spirit energy to replace it.

Reflection Questions

1. What goals consume your energy and attention?

2. Read Philippians 3:12–14 again and define, as specifically
as you know it, that for which Christ Jesus took hold of you.

3. Has the Spirit identified any sin patterns still active in you?
What behaviors do you use to earn love and approval?

4. Would you specifically release those patterns to God and confess to Him that you have trusted partially in yourself and not totally in Him? Receive His forgiveness. Let the Spirit train you in "the new way of the Spirit, not the old way of the law."

5. Begin now to neglect the old ways. Leave them behind. Press on toward the goal.

Experience 2

Beside each phrase, write what it means to you. Add Scripture references that come to mind. Finally, restate the Scripture and describe any visual thoughts.

(Phil. 3:12–14)
I press on

to take hold of that for which
Christ Jesus took hold of me. . . .

Forgetting what is behind

and straining toward that
what is ahead,

I press on toward the goal

to win the prize

for which God has called me
heavenward in Christ Jesus.

Restate the Scripture:

Visual thoughts:

Experience 3

What questions does this Scripture answer?

"I press on to take hold of that for which Christ Jesus took hold of me. . . . Forgetting what is behind and straining toward what is ahead, I press on toward the goal to win the prize for which God has called me heavenward in Christ Jesus" (Phil. 3:12–14).

Experience 4

What is God saying to you?

Experience 5

What is your response to Him?

Experience 6

What promises has God made to you from His Word? Write them down. Beside each, write the name(s) of the person(s) for whom you prayed this promise and the date you prayed.

Experience 7

Write out faith statements.

Worship with abandon!

THE WISE HEART

Experience 1

"Since a king's word is supreme, who can say to him, 'What are you doing?' Whoever obeys his command will come to no harm, and the wise heart will know the proper time and procedure. For there is a proper time and procedure for every matter" *(Eccl. 8:4–6).*

God tells us many times in His Word that He is supreme and that it is foolish of us to question His judgment. He doesn't say we shouldn't ask Him questions. He says we shouldn't challenge His wisdom. "Since a king's word is supreme, who can say to him, 'What are you doing?'" (Eccl. 8:4).

> "But who are you, O man, to talk back to God? 'Shall what is formed say to him who formed it, "Why did you make me like this?"' Does not the potter have the right to make out of the same lump of clay some pottery for noble purposes and some for common use?" (Rom. 9:20–21).

> "You turn things upside down, as if the potter were thought to be like the clay! Shall what is formed say to him who formed it, 'He did not make me?' Can the pot say of the potter, 'He knows nothing'?" (Isa. 29:16).

> "He does as he pleases with the powers of heaven and the peoples of the earth. No one can hold back his

hand or say to him: 'What have you done?'"
(Dan. 4:35).

When we understand that He is supreme in heaven and on earth, and that in His supremacy He desires the highest good for each of us, then we will not balk when He says, "Don't question My wisdom. It will be only foolishness on your part." As He is leading us along the best path, He may give commands that appear on the surface to call for foolish or reckless action from us.

Simon Peter, experienced fisherman, worked hard all night trying to catch fish and caught none. Jesus, not a fisherman, said, "'Put out into deep water, and let down the nets for a catch'" (Luke 5:4). Peter thought it seemed foolish. He decided, though, to humor Jesus and, without enthusiasm or expectations, obeyed. As a result, "He and all his companions were astonished at the catch of fish they had taken"
(Luke 5:9).

Jesus said to a paralytic who lay at His feet unable to move, "'I tell you, get up, take your mat and go home.'" What a foolish command it must have seemed. Had the man not tried to walk before, only to find himself unable to move a muscle? Yet, "immediately he stood up in front of them, took what he had been lying on and went home praising God"
(Luke 5:22–25).

Feed a crowd of more than 5,000 people with five loaves of bread and two fish. Walk on the water. Leave your livelihood and follow Me. Forgive your enemies. Be a servant. Lay down your life. Followers of Jesus will hear many commands that could appear reckless, but the Word teaches us that we are the foolish ones if we question His wisdom. The King's command is supreme.

The Power to Obey

Once we learn to trust His wisdom implicitly, His commands no longer have the ring of foolishness to them. Reckless obedience to His voice is what He is looking for. When He finds a person of uncompromising obedience, who doesn't hesitate for fear of the consequences, He pours out His power in that one. The one who has learned that "whoever obeys his command will come to no harm" (Eccl. 8:5), can leave the consequences in the King's hands and obey fearlessly.

God doesn't give foolish commands. They only seem foolish when evaluated with human wisdom. He deals with you wisely, always careful over you and mindful of your humanness. He doesn't require anything He is not willing to supply. "I, the Lord, have called you in righteousness; I will take hold of your hand" (Isa. 42:6). When He commands, He provides the power to obey.

When He commands, He doesn't send you out on your own to obey. He is closer than "with you"; He is in you. His energy is working mightily in you (Col. 1:29).

The Wisdom to Obey

"The wise heart will know the proper time and procedure" (Eccl. 8:5). When God gives you an assignment, He doesn't lay it all out at once. He leads us in a way that will require our constant attention. He leads step-by-step, obedience by obedience. "Today, if you hear His voice, do not harden your heart."

As you are obeying Him, He reveals wisdom as you need it. The wise heart will know what it needs to know when it needs to know it. God will make the right thing known at the right time. He leads as you go.

> "'I will lead the blind by ways they have not known, along unfamiliar paths I will guide them; I will turn the darkness into light before them and make the rough places smooth. These are things I will do; I will not forsake them'" (Isa. 42:16).

God promises that He will lead you as if He were leading a blind person along unfamiliar paths. A blind person can manage well along familiar paths, but has no way to safely navigate unfamiliar paths. One who is leading a blind person by ways he has not known will be guiding and directing each step, each movement. The guide will be moving obstacles and smoothing the way. The guide will not leave the blind person on his own even momentarily. The guide will be protecting the blind person from dangers he cannot see.

The blind person will rely on the sight of his guide. He will put all his trust in his guide. As long as the blind person is in the guide's care, his disability does not limit him. He is tapping into the guide's ability and that's all he needs.

As you obey God's commands, all you have to do is rely fully on Him. Your inability does not matter. God doesn't shrink the size of His power to fit within your abilities; He expands your abilities to accommodate the size of His power. His power is most visible in your weakness. As Paul says, rejoice in your weaknesses—embrace them, celebrate them. They are the perfect background against which God can display His power. Your weaknesses will complement His power perfectly.

Reckless Obedience Is Perfectly Safe

"Whoever obeys his command will come to no harm" (Eccl. 8:5). "The way of the Lord is a refuge for the righteous" (Prov. 10:29). When you are following His way, the way He is directing you is a refuge.

God will work patiently and gently with you as you struggle to the point of obedience when His call looks risky or difficult. Jesus had to struggle through His human fears to reach the point of calm and serenity that He displayed during His trial and humiliation. He reached the point where he could confront the danger because of the surpassing value of the ultimate goal. He entrusted Himself to the Father, safe in the knowledge that no one has power over Him. So don't fear the struggle. Only when you refuse to be obedient have you moved out of the way of the Lord. Time and experience will teach you this: Sometimes you will enter into obedience say-ing, "Do I have to?" But in the center of obedience you will always find yourself saying, "Do I get to?" Every time you struggle through to obedience, you'll say, "Thank You, Father, for getting me here. Imagine what I'd have missed if I had given in to fear and refused Your voice." Obedience becomes easier as you build a history with the Father.

When you are obeying His commands, you will know what you need to know when you need to know it.

Reflection Questions

1. Have you challenged the King's command? If so, are you willing to repent of your disobedience and obey Him now?

2. Can you remember a time in the past when you obeyed Him recklessly? What was the result?

3. Is fear holding you back? Describe any command that you are struggling with right now.

4. Do you honestly believe that when you are on a mission for the King, you will know what you need to know when you need to know it?

5. Will you move forward in obedience?

Experience 2

Beside each phrase, write what it means to you. Add Scripture references that come to mind. Restate the Scripture and describe any visual thoughts.

(Eccl. 8:4–6)
Since a king's word
is supreme,

who can say to him,
"What are you doing?"

Whoever obeys his
command

will come to no harm,

and the wise heart

will know the proper
time and procedure.

For there is a proper time
and procedure for every matter.

Restate the Scripture:

Visual thoughts:

Experience 3

What questions does this Scripture answer?

"Since a king's word is supreme, who can say to him, 'What are you doing?' Whoever obeys his command will come to no harm, and the wise heart will know the proper time and procedure. For there is a proper time and procedure for every matter" (Eccl. 8:4–6).

Experience 4

What is God saying to you?

Experience 5

What is your response to Him?

Experience 6

What promises has God made to you from His Word? Write them down. Beside each, write the name(s) of the person(s) for whom you prayed this promise and the date you prayed.

Experience 7
Write out faith statements.

Worship with abandon!

SET YOUR HEART

Experience 1

"Set your hearts on things above, where Christ is seated at the right hand of God. Set your minds on things above, not on earthly things" (Col. 3:1–2). (Focal passage: Col. 3:1–17)

"So we fix our eyes not on what is seen, but on what is unseen" (2 Cor. 4:18).

Recently I read a report from a group of scientists who were studying the rate at which the physical senses mature. They conducted an experiment in which crawling babies were being studied for depth perception. The babies were placed on a flat, level floor. The floor was a black-and-white checkerboard pattern. At a certain place in the floor, the checkerboard pattern changed. The black-and-white alternating squares became progressively smaller. This gave the visual illusion of a sudden steep drop-off. None of the babies would come near the place they perceived as the edge.

As I read this report, I thought, *How like us!* These babies were acting on their immature, uninformed perceptions of reality. Because they did not know about optical illusions, their activity was limited and restricted to a small area, when in reality they had a large space in which to safely play. If only they had known the truth, they would have been free to expand their horizons; but they were immature and unable to make judgments based on anything except appearance.

We too are inclined to feel safer if we base our actions and beliefs on what we can directly observe. We place great faith in

the information our physical senses gather. We look at circumstances on the earth and mistake them for the full truth. We
allow our earthbound perceptions to define our sense of reality. We limit ourselves by settling for what appears to be true.

The Word warns us against such a limiting and sense-
based definition of reality. Jesus said "'Stop judging by mere
appearances, and make a right judgment'" (John 7:24). He
was speaking to people who were basing their behavior on
outward, rule-following, formula obedience and were blind
to the spirit and intent of God's law. He was trying to help
them see that God was not limiting them, but that they were
limiting themselves. They were lacking depth perception.
They accepted the outward form as if it were the essence.
They treated the journey as if it were the destination. They
believed the illusion.

The Truth Sets Free

Jesus said in John 8:32 that the truth sets people free. "'If you
hold to my teaching, you are really my disciples. Then you
will know the truth, and the truth will set you free'"(John
8:31–32). Jesus says that knowing the truth will set you free.
To know means to understand or fully comprehend. The
word translated "truth" means the true essence that underlies
the appearance. Truth is what lies beneath the veneer; truth is
the substance. The word translated "truth" could also be
translated "reality."

What did Jesus say about reality? He said only those who
hold to and continue in His teaching would recognize and
understand it. He said only those who do understand the
reality beneath the surface appearance will be free. In other
words, freedom comes from living in harmony with reality.
Living by appearance rather than truth is limiting. God's plan
is not to limit, but to expand. "He reached down from on
high and took hold of me. . . . He brought me out into a spacious place" (Psalm 18:16,19). "You broaden the path
beneath me, so that my ankles do not turn" (Psalm 18:36).

The person without the Spirit of God is limited to knowing and understanding what is observable with the physical senses. Since reality consists of what we *can see* as well as what we *can't see*, this person cannot see the whole picture. This person can only see appearance.

Appearance is misleading. For example, based on appearance, one would conclude that the sun revolves around the earth. This has every appearance of being true, so an uninformed person would mistake it for truth. It requires a knowledge of factors that are not directly observable to perceive the truth. When the perception of truth is narrowly drawn, based on appearance, then behavior is unrealistic because it is guided by an illusion. When behavior does not correspond to reality, then a person is restricted and limited instead of being free. Remember the babies in the study. Their immature understanding caused them to restrict themselves.

In Plato's work, *The Republic,* we find a parable that, despite its original intent, well describes the difference between living by appearance and living by truth. I will condense it for you. It goes something like this:

> Picture a race of men who live in an underground cave-dwelling. This race of men have lived in this cave all their lives. Not only do they live underground, but their necks and legs are bound by chains in such a way that they cannot change positions or turn their heads. They are facing a cave wall, and it is all of the world they have ever seen. Some distance behind them, and higher up, a huge fire is burning. Between the fire and the chained men lives another race of men. This race moves and lives in such a way that the light from the fire casts their shadows on the cave wall.
>
> The chained men have seen nothing of reality except the shadows cast on the cave wall. The acoustics in the cave would cause it to seem that voices were coming from the shadows. The only truth they know is really shadow. They believe

shadow to be substance because they have never seen the substance.

Imagine that one of these bound men one day broke the chains, stood up, and began to walk toward the light. His eyes, never having been exposed to light, would first have to adjust to the light before he could see the objects that had been casting the shadows. After his period of adjustment to the light, he would begin to see substance for the first time. When he realizes that everything he knows and believes is really shadow, does he not consider himself blessed to be so enlightened? Does finding light and substance more than make up for the shadow existence he has left behind?

If I am going to define truth based on what I can observe with my senses, my entire existence will be defined by a misunderstanding. I will be limited and disoriented. I will believe shadow to be substance. If I look at the circumstances on earth and believe them to be the only solid reality, I will never know the fullness and completeness that Jesus offers.

Do you see why God wants us to know reality? Do you see that He longs for us to be uninhibited and free so that we can achieve our potential? He does not want us to be held captive by conjecture and assumption. He wants us to be free to live abundantly. He wants to show you the rock-solid reality that underlies the appearance. He wants you to know and understand the truth.

The Eternal v. the Temporal

Paul said, "Set your heart on things above." When you have your heart set on something, how does it affect you? You pursue that goal. Nothing else will satisfy you. You lay aside everything that distracts you.

Think about the Olympic athletes. The media focuses on athletes who have their hearts set on making the Olympic teams. As we hear the athletes' stories, we admire their dedication, their sacrifices, their single-minded pursuit of a consuming dream. We wonder at their drive and resiliency, as many of them have overcome seemingly insurmountable obstacles or bounced back from defeats that would have caused someone less focused to give up. They have set their hearts.

This is how I picture Paul and his challenge to us. We must set our hearts on things above: on the realities that cannot be seen with earthly eyes, on the things that Jesus is dispensing from His seat at the Father's right hand, and on what Jesus is doing in every circumstance. Refuse distractions. Turn away from the shadow; embrace the substance. You cannot know the truth of a matter until you have taken into account the things above.

Don't focus your eyes on what you can see—the circumstances of earth. Instead, focus your eyes on the facts and realities of the spiritual realm—the sovereignty of God, the authority of Jesus, the power of the Spirit. Let your spiritual senses mature until you have spiritual depth perception and can experience life in God's spacious place.

Reflection Questions

1. What circumstances on earth are causing you anxiety? Describe them as they appear.

2. Now, set your mind on things above. Let the Spirit show you the spiritual aspect of reality as it relates to these circumstances. Describe the circumstances again—this time from the Spirit's perspective.

3. What difference will it make in you if you start focusing on the spiritual reality instead of restricting your focus to the earthly?

Experience 2

Beside each phrase, write what it means to you. Add Scripture references that come to mind. Restate the Scripture and describe any visual thoughts.

(**Col. 3:1–2**)
Set your hearts

on things above,

where Christ is seated
at the right hand of God.

Set your minds

on things above,

not on earthly things.

So we fix our eyes

not on what is seen,

but on what is unseen.

Restate the Scripture:

Visual thoughts:

Experience 3

What questions do these Scriptures answer?

"Set your hearts on things above, where Christ is seated at the right hand of God. Set your minds on things above, not on earthly things" (Col. 3:1–2).

"So we fix our eyes not on what is seen, but on what is unseen" (2 Cor. 4:18).

Experience 4

What is God saying to you?

Experience 5

What is your response to Him?

Experience 6

What promises has God made to you from His Word? Write them down. Beside each, write the name(s) of the person(s) for whom you prayed this promise and the date you prayed.

Experience 7

Write out faith statements.

Worship with abandon!

THE LORD'S PURPOSE PREVAILS

Experience 1

"The lot is cast into the lap, but its every decision is from the Lord" (Prov. 16:33).

"Many are the plans in a man's heart, but it is the Lord's purpose that prevails" (Prov. 19:21).

God is in the details. One of the most important truths God has woven into His Word is that He is engineering even the smallest detail in order to establish His divine purpose in every situation. "The lot is cast into the lap, but its every decision is from the Lord" (Prov. 16:33). Happenings that seem random, choices and decisions that seem spontaneous and uncalculated, paths that cross in a seemingly serendipitous way—all are being put in order by the Lord. "The steps of a man are established by the Lord; and He delights in his way. When he falls, he shall not be hurled headlong; because the Lord is the one who holds his hand" (Psalm 37:23–24 NASB).

Does anything seem more random than the casting of a lot? Yet the Scripture teaches us that even what seems unplanned or uncontrolled—a lot cast into the lap—is really being ordered by the Lord. In fact, God used the casting of lots to express His will in many situations in the Old Covenant. The land of Caanan was distributed among the 12 tribes by casting lots. "The Lord said to Moses, . . . 'Be sure that the land is distributed by lot'" (Num. 26:52,55). Yet we know that God Himself assigned each tribe its parcel of land. He gave it to them as an inheritance. "He . . . allotted their lands to them as an inheritance; he settled the tribes of Israel in their homes" (Psalm 78:55).

When we are living in covenant relationship with the Most High God, Ruler of heaven and earth, nothing—not one detail—is random. God, in His Word, points us to His ways. "I meditate on your precepts and consider your ways" (Psalm 119:15). He tells us to consider His ways, learn His ways, observe His ways. The word *way* in this context means a well-worn path. God tells us to observe and learn His consistent methods of dealing with situations and people. When we know His ways, recognize the underlying consistency in all His doings, we will learn to see the divine will in the center of everything. It is His way to manage the details, to act according to an eternal plan. "I will exalt you and praise your name, for in perfect faithfulness you have done marvelous things, things planned long ago" (Isa. 25:1). Whatever is happening in your life right now, even though it may seem out of control, even though it may seem as if circumstances are taking on a momentum of their own, God is acting according to a plan that has been in place since the beginning of time. It may look as if the lot has been randomly cast in your lap, but remember—its every decision is from the Lord.

God's Prevailing Purpose

"Many are the plans in a man's heart, but it is the Lord's purpose that prevails" (Prov. 19:21). Man's thoughts and intentions are not hidden from God's view. "Nothing in all creation is hidden from God's sight. Everything is uncovered and laid bare before the eyes of him to whom we must give account" (Heb. 4:13). The plans in a person's innermost being, even before those thoughts are fully formed, are known by God. Before a thought has fully evolved into a conscious thought—before it has taken the form of words— God knows it thoroughly. "Before a word is on my tongue you know it completely, O Lord" (Psalm 139:4). God knows the thoughts of all people, even those who are hostile to Him. "[Jesus] did not need man's testimony about man, for he knew what was in a man" (John 2:25). He is able to use even the thoughts and plans in the heart of a person—both believers and unbelievers—to bring about His divine purposes.

Have you ever thought about how detailed and exactly timed the arrest, trial, crucifixion, burial, and resurrection of Jesus was? The exact timing had been established before the world began. God gave an elaborate and explicit picture of the timing when He established the feasts in the Old Covenant, generations before the event occurred in history. Jesus had to be on the cross and dead by sundown on Passover because He is the Paschal Lamb. The exact incident had to occur by twilight on the 14th day of the first month, the month of Nisan. He had to be in the ground before 6:00 P.M. because He is the whole burnt offering sacrifice for the nation. He had to be in the ground three days and three nights because He was prophesied to by Jonah in the belly of the whale. He had to be resurrected on the third day, the day following the Sabbath, the Feast of Firstfruits, because He is the Firstfruits of the Spirit. He had to be resurrected after sunset and before sunrise. Every detail of His ordeal was laid out in the beginning. God's timetable was exact. He did not deviate from it at all.

However, look at the events that put everything on this timetable. "Now the Feast of Unleavened Bread, called the Passover, was approaching, and chief priests and the teachers of the law were looking for some way to get rid of Jesus, for they were afraid of the people" (Luke 22:1–2). At exactly the right moment, Jesus' enemies began to act on their festering hatred and fear of Him. Until that moment, Jesus had always said, "My time is not yet come." Until that time, His enemies' schemes could not succeed.

Because of their impatience to finish the deed before the Sabbath, Jesus' enemies called an unusual meeting of the Sanhedrin, then they woke Pilate, then Herod (who just happened to be in Jerusalem at that time), and finally Pilate again. What should have taken several days was railroaded through by enemies of God. Because of their manipulation of events, every event occurred exactly on God's predetermined timetable, the timetable He had planned from the beginning of time and announced early in Israel's history.

"The Lord works out everything for his own ends—even the wicked for a day of disaster" (Prov. 16:4). Even Satan is nothing more than a pawn in God's hands. Observe Satan's part in God's plan: Between the temptation of Jesus and His crucifixion, Satan was watching for a perfect time to carry out his own agenda. "When the devil had finished all this tempting, he left him until an opportune time" (Luke 4:13). Now—at this exact moment—Satan sees his opportune time. "Satan entered Judas. . . . And Judas went to the chief priests and the officers of the temple guard and discussed with them how he might betray Jesus. . . . He . . . watched for an opportunity to hand Jesus over to them when no crowd was present" (Luke 22:3–5). Satan had found the opportune time for which he had been watching. The irony is that it was God's opportune time, not Satan's.

Through every page of Scripture God shows us His ways. He uses everything to work out His own purposes. His purpose will prevail no matter what plans are in the hearts of men. Every one of God's enemies, though they plotted and fought against His people, became the means to His end. You and I, His children who are in covenant relationship with Him, are never at the mercy of any person or any circumstance. God is never taken by surprise at any person's decisions or actions. He has already factored them into His purpose and plan for us.

Rest in the fact that God is managing every detail in order to work out His purposes. "All the ways of the Lord are loving and faithful" (Psalm 25:10). Nothing is left to chance.

Reflection Questions

1. Is there any circumstance in your life right now that seems to be careening out of control? Perhaps it is a circumstance that was brought on by wrong and ungodly decisions.

2. As you meditate on God's Word today, do you believe that God has lost control? Do you think that anything or anyone can thwart Him?

3. Do you believe that any plan or any purpose can succeed against the Lord? "There is no wisdom, no insight, no plan that can succeed against the Lord" (Prov. 21:30).

4. Thank God that He is working out His purpose in the midst of circumstances that look like undirected chaos. Commit to Him that you will begin now to deal with these circumstances with your mind set on Him.

Experience 2

Beside each phrase, write what it means to you. Add Scripture references that come to mind. Restate the Scriptures and describe any visual thoughts.

(Prov. 16:33)
The lot is cast into
the lap,

but its every decision
is from the Lord.

(Prov. 19:21)
Many are the plans
in a man's heart,

but it is the Lord's
purpose that prevails.

Restate the Scripture:

Visual thoughts:

Experience 3

What questions do these Scriptures answer?

"The lot is cast into the lap, but its every decision is from the Lord" (Prov. 16:33).

"Many are the plans in a man's heart, but it is the Lord's purpose that prevails" (Prov. 19:21)

Experience 4

What is God saying to you?

Experience 5

What is your response to Him?

Experience 6

What promises has God made to you from His Word? Write them down. Beside each, write the name(s) of the person(s) for whom you prayed this promise and the date you prayed.

Experience 7

Write out faith statements.

Worship with abandon!

THE INVISIBLE WORK

Experience 1

"'This is what the kingdom of God is like. A man scatters seed on the ground. Night and day, whether he sleeps or gets up, the seed sprouts and grows, though he does not know how. All by itself the soil produces grain—first the stalk, then the head, then the full kernel in the head. As soon as the grain is ripe, he puts the sickle to it, because the harvest has come'" (Mark 4:26–29).

God's kingdom works on a principle that I call the principle of progressive revelation. If you look closely at God's work from Genesis through Revelation, His work in your life, His work in the lives of others, you will see that nothing springs forth full-grown. Everything in the material creation and everything in the spiritual realm is progressively revealed. For this reason, it requires both faith and patience to receive your inheritance—the promises. "We do not want you to become lazy, but to imitate those who through faith and patience inherit what has been promised. . . . And so after waiting patiently, Abraham received what was promised" (Heb. 6:12,15).

Faith is the ability to know for certain what you cannot observe with your physical senses. (See Heb. 11:1.) The word translated "patience" is more accurately translated "long-suffering." It suggests a tranquil soul, a sedate mind, an unruffled attitude toward difficulty, a steadiness of purpose.

The promises that are your inheritance—your certain possession—will not come into your life full-grown. The promises to which the writer of Hebrews is referring are not generic promises, but specific promises to individuals. God promised Abraham specifically: "'I will surely bless you and give you many descendants'" (Heb. 6:14). Yet this promise was progressively unfolded. God did not make the promise and fulfill the promise on the same day. A long period of time elapsed between the promise and its fulfillment. Abraham had to exercise faith and patience before the fulfillment of the promise entered his experience.

Abraham's faith journey was much like the farmer's experience in Jesus' parable. When the seed was planted—when Abram entered into covenant with God and combined his faith with God's promise[1]—a long period ensued that appeared from the earth perspective to be desultory. Weeks, months, years, decades passed with no sign of the promised heir. God was working. We see it clearly in retrospect. But His work was underground; His work was invisible to the physical eye. Yet that period of invisible activity was bringing about exactly the right setting, exactly the right time, and exactly the right heart to put the promise on the earth at the opportune moment. When that moment arrived, that exactly right predetermined moment, the stalk appeared—Isaac was born. Then the head appeared—the nation of Israel grew more numerous than the sands on the seashore or the stars in the sky. Then the full kernel in the head—the Messiah was born and brought salvation and redemption.

Abraham was "still living by faith when [he] died. [He] did not receive the things promised; [he] only saw them and welcomed them from a distance" (Heb. 11:13). Abraham received what was promised directly to him—an heir and a land—but he did not receive the fully developed promise.

The promises still enter our lives in the same way that God's promise to Abraham entered his life. First the seed; then the waiting and training period during which we exercise faith and patience; then the stalk; the head; and finally, the full kernel in the head. This is God's pattern and He never deviates from it. He never acts like a vending machine or an instant scratch-and-win game. His purpose is too far-reaching, His plans are too long-term, His riches are too precious for Him to throw them at us like confetti. He must prepare the ground in which the promise will grow. As the fulfilled promises appear in our experience, they are well rooted and fully nourished because of the faith and patience that has fertilized them.

When the farmer plants the seed, he anticipates the harvest. When God's specific promises come into your life, we anticipate their fulfillment. God performs with His hand what He promises. He keeps covenant. It is impossible for Him to lie. The farmer could miss the harvest only one way: by leaving his field behind. He might grow impatient with the process and decide that the seed would not really produce the plant. He might imagine that he could get a quicker harvest somewhere else. He might decide that it's easier to buy someone else's harvest instead of waiting on his own. The harvest would come, but he would not be available to put the sickle to it.

God's Invisible Work

It's easy for us to misunderstand the interaction between the spiritual realm—the invisible aspects of reality—and the material and physical realm—the tangible aspects of reality. We might think that God's work in the material realm, His work in getting the promise into our earthly experience, is the primary work. This thinking is exactly the reverse of the truth. The warfare and the work do not occur in the material realm. Putting His resources into our lives at precisely the right time and in precisely the right way presents no difficulty for Him. The warfare and the work occur in the spiritual realm. He has ordained prayer as the way we will cooperate with Him as He does His spiritual, inside, underground work. As soon as the spiritual work is done, the material manifestation of the promise appears on earth.

This time of unobservable work, this time during which the seed is germinating, is a time of activity and a time in which God's power is operating mightily. We will only know this work by faith because faith is what connects our earthly minds to spiritual reality. Don't mistake the appearance of inactivity for God's delay. He is not delaying; He is working in the invisible realm.

Reflection Questions
1. What promise(s) has God given you that has been long in coming?

2. In your memory, go back to a time when you were certain about the promise. Write down how you felt about the promise at that time.

3. Have you become discouraged as the time has passed? Describe your feelings about the promise right now.

4. What has God said to you as you have thought through this devotional?

5. Have you left the ground where the seed was planted to pursue other possibilities?

6. Take time with the Father today. Let Him refresh the promise for you, as He did so often with Abraham.

7. If the Father never did another specific or tangible thing for you while you live on the earth, would you still love Him with all your heart? Do you firmly believe that the most important promise He ever made, the indwelling life of the Son, is completely fulfilled in you? Say to Him right now, "My soul is satisfied with abundance." Let His Spirit in you make this attitude reality.

Experience 2

Beside each phrase, write what it means to you. Add Scripture references that come to mind. Restate the Scripture and describe any visual thoughts.

(**Mark 4:26–29**)
This is what the kingdom
of God is like.

A man scatters seeds on
the ground.

Night and day, whether
he sleeps or gets up,

the seed sprouts and grows,

though he does not know how.

All by itself the soil produces
grain—

first the stalk, then the head,
then the full kernel in the head.

As soon as the grain is ripe,

he puts the sickle to it,

because the harvest has come.

Restate the Scripture:

Visual thoughts:

Experience 3

What questions does this Scripture answer?

"'This is what the kingdom of God is like. A man scatters seed on the ground. Night and day, whether he sleeps or gets up, the seed sprouts and grows, though he does not know how. All by itself the soil produces grain—first the stalk, then the head, then the full kernel in the head. As soon as the grain is ripe, he puts the sickle to it, because the harvest has come'" (Mark 4:26–29).

Experience 4

What is God saying to you?

Experience 5

What is your response to Him?

Experience 6

What promises has God made to you from His Word? Write them down. Beside each, write the name(s) of the persons for whom you prayed this promise and the date you prayed.

Experience 7

Write out faith statements.

Worship with abandon!

[1]Hebrews 4:2 says, "But the message they heard was of no value to them, because those who heard did not combine it with faith." Until the promise of God is combined with the faith of a person, it is inactive. The combining of promise and faith creates a seed—a life carrier—that will grow into fulfillment.

MOUNTAINS BECOME ROADS

Experience 1

"I will turn all my mountains into roads, and my highways will be raised up" (Isa. 49:11). (Focal passage: Isa. 49:8–13)

God knows no obstacles. Nothing can obstruct or interrupt His plan for you. Nothing impedes His progress in you. Do not look at earth's roadblocks as having the final say. God will take obstacles and make them into roads. He will raise up ditches so that they become level ground.

The Word pictures two types of obstructions: one a natural part of the landscape, the other a man-made highway. Neither, He declares, will stand in His way.

Stumbling Blocks Become Stepping-Stones

In nature, a mountain represents a barrier. When a mountain stands between a traveler and his destination, he must find a way past it. The traveler will have to go around it, lengthening his journey and delaying his arrival; or he will have to climb it, exhausting his physical strength and delaying his arrival. Either way, a mountain stands in the way of the traveler's progress.

In this passage of Scripture, a mountain represents a naturally occurring hindrance. When you encounter a hindrance on your spiritual journey of following God's will, do not be discouraged. Even a hindrance that seems to be part of life's landscape, inescapable and unchangeable, will not stop you. Follow God. He will make that mountain into a road. He will use that very obstacle to get you where you're going. It will become the means to His end. He will not bless you in spite of difficulties, but by means of them.

In this same passage, God refers to a highway. A highway was a man-made road created by throwing dirt up along the two sides so that a ditchlike path was created. God says that the highways will be raised up, made level, so that no traveler will stumble into them or be deterred by them. When you encounter difficulties that seem to have been engineered by human beings, even by human beings who are not following God, do not be discouraged. God is sovereign even over the activities and plans of His enemies. Every roadblock will turn out to your advantage.

Once we learn to depend on Him alone, we have nothing left to fear. When our thoughts are fixed on Him, He keeps us in uninterrupted peace. He does not promise that we will encounter no mountains. He says we will be confronted by mountains, but that He will make them into roads. He does not promise we will not come across ditches in our journeys. He says we will, but He will raise them up and make them level ground. He doesn't tell us we won't encounter difficulty. Instead, He says not to fear difficulty when we do encounter it. "'In this world you will have trouble. But take heart! I have overcome the world'" (John 16:33).

God's Uses for Obstacles

Nothing comes into your life without God's permission. He only allows into your life those situations and circumstances that will move you forward toward the goal. You never have to wonder whether a situation is from God or from some other source. No matter the immediate source, God's sovereign care for you is in effect at all times.

Hannah Whithall Smith, in her book, *The God of All Comfort,* addresses our attitude toward difficulties like this:

He may not have ordered them, but He is in them somewhere, and He is in them to compel, even the most grievous, to work together for our good. The "second causes" of the wrong may be full of malice and wickedness, but faith never sees second causes. It sees only the hand of God behind the second causes. They are all under His control, and not one of them can touch us except with His knowledge and permission. The thing itself that happens cannot perhaps be said to be the will of God, but by the time its effects reach us they have become God's will for us, and must be accepted as from His hands.[1]

God is working out His good and perfect will through every situation that arises. He uses difficulties and obstacles in productive ways.

God's plans are perfectly timed. The time for God's plan to take effect has been determined by Him and His timing is crucial. Sometimes God gives His permission for an obstacle to enter your life in order to keep you from taking an action before the timing is right. If an obstacle is able to stand, it is because God has ordained it to stand—for a time.

Sometimes God allows hindrances to spring up in order to keep you from taking a wrong step. If a hindrance is able to stop you from moving forward in a certain direction, it is because God is protecting you from a mistake. Your spiritual sense of sight is not as mature as it will be later, so God is keeping you from acting on something that appears to be from Him, but is only an illusion.

God uses obstacles in your path to refocus your faith. Moments of crisis can cause you to recognize that other things have moved in and diluted pure faith in God. These situations can cause you to see that, without being aware of it, you have transferred some of your trust to other people or to institutions or to your own abilities. When God graciously allows these situations to stop you in your tracks, suddenly you see that everything you've been trusting in is useless. God draws your faith back to Himself as He reminds you that He alone is absolutely trustworthy.

God often uses mountains on your journey to strengthen and mature your faith. When you are on your faith walk, steadily moving forward by God's power, and suddenly a mountain looms, God looks you in the eye, takes your face in His hands, and says, "Will you trust Me?" Those words resonate through your spirit and faith rises up to say, "Yes, Lord, I will trust You." Then you find that as you keep moving forward, one step at a time, the mountain turns into a road before you. The more mountain-into-road experiences God takes you through, the less any mountain will intimidate you.

God sometimes allows mountains in your path in order to affirm your direction. When mountains turn into roads before you and highways are raised up to meet you, God is affirming that "this is the way, walk in it."

Look at the Scripture we are examining. What does God call the mountains? He calls them "my mountains." What does God call the highways? He calls them "my highways." When mountains and highways are in your path, who claims responsibility for them? Your loving Father does.

Who will turn the mountains into roads? He will. Who will raise up the highways? He will. When you see a mountain in your path, look again. It is the loving and powerful hand of the Almighty.

Reflection Questions

1. What mountains or highways are in your path right now?

2. Do you recall any time when God has made a mountain into a road for you?

3. What has been your attitude about the obstacle in your path right now?

4. To the best of your ability to discern, what do you sense is God's purpose for leaving the current obstacle in place? Is it to:
- control the timing?
- keep you from taking a wrong step?
- refocus your faith?
- strengthen and mature your faith?

5. Is God causing you to see the obstacles in your life differently? How?

Experience 2

Beside each phrase, write what it means to you. Add Scripture references that come to mind. Restate the Scripture and describe any visual thoughts.

(Isa. 49:11)
I will turn all
my mountains

into roads,

and my highways

will be raised up.

Restate the Scripture:

Visual thoughts:

Experience 3

What questions does this Scripture answer?

"I will turn all my mountains into roads, and my highways will be raised up" (Isa. 49:11).

Experience 4

What is God saying to you?

Experience 5

What is your response to Him?

Experience 6

What promises has God made to you from His Word? Write them down. Beside each, write the name(s) of the person(s) for whom you prayed this promise and the date you prayed.

Experience 7

Write out faith statements.

Worship with abandon!

[1]Hannah Whithall Smith, *The God of All Comfort* (Uhrichsville, OH: Barbour and Company, Inc., 1984), 164.

MOVING ON

As you worked through this devotional book, you learned and practiced methods for contemplative prayer based on the Word. You may have found some of the methods to be productive for you and other methods not as well suited to your personality. You may have started developing your own derivations of some of the methods or maybe you have created methods that are uniquely yours.

I believe that you have learned several important foundational truths.

- God's Word is full and running over with wisdom, knowledge, and insight.
- God Himself is willing and eager to teach you His Word.
- You have as much ability to hear from God as anyone who has ever lived or will ever live.
- God speaks the written Word through the Living Word.

Don't stop now. Continue to develop your own journaling and prayer methods. Continue learning how to delve into the riches stored in secret places. Press on toward the goal.

I imagine that God has used His Word to create an insatiable appetite for Him. I encourage you to feed that craving continually. Don't allow your freshly stirred hunger to slacken. Continue diligently in His Word.

> Deep within us all there is an amazing inner sanctuary of the soul, a holy place, a Divine Center, a speaking voice, to which we may continually return.

Eternity is at our hearts, pressing upon our time-torn lives, warming us with intimations of an astounding destiny, calling us home unto Itself. . . . It is a seed stirring to life if we do not choke it. It is the Shekinah of the soul, the Presence in the midst.[1]

The Shekinah of the soul is now burning continually in you. Learn to stoke its fires; never let the flame recede.

Your holy Fire now burns within
And purges every secret sin.
My life the bush, Your Life the Flame
That leaves me nevermore the same.

Your life in me ignites the Fire
That now fulfills my heart's desire.
The Spirit's work, my life made new
Transformed within, ablaze with You.[2]

Suggestions for using *Riches Stored in Secret Places* with small groups, prayer partners, discipleship/Bible study groups, Sunday School classes, and in one-on-one mentoring relationships

Each person should have his or her own copy of *Riches Stored in Secret Places*. You can purchase copies at your local Christian bookstore, or order by calling 1 (800) 968-7301.

Decide how and when you want to meet together. Before your first meeting, each participant should prayerfully read "Getting Started" on pages 1–9. Ask participants to notice what concepts appeal to them most. Encourage them to underline sentences or Scripture references that speak to their own longings.

Introductory Meeting
1. Commit to each other that you will meet together 12 times. Be sure participants understand that they will never

have to share their private journal entries or honest responses unless they want to and feel comfortable doing so.

2. Discuss how participants felt about "Getting Started." Discussion starters might be:

What is it about this devotional experience that attracts you?

Do you have any reservations about committing to this devotional journey?

What is it that you are longing for God to do in your life?

3. If you are a group, ask participants if they would like to partner with another group member for the duration of this experience. Partners could agree to support each other daily in prayer, asking the Father to speak powerfully. Partners might want to plan to talk briefly each week for support and to share new insights and discoveries.

a) If group members want to work as partners, stop and assign partners now. Partner women with women and men with men, unless married couples want to be each other's partner.

b) Ask partners to spend several minutes together. They should decide how they will encourage one another.

c) Ask partners to exchange phone numbers, fax numbers, email addresses, and mailing addresses.

d) Ask each partner to share one overall prayer request for the 12-week experience (for example, "What do you want God to do in you through this experience?"). Partners should agree to pray for each other's request regularly.

4. Talk through the format and be sure that everyone understands it. Emphasize that there will be no assignment checks or tests. The goal of this book is to help you go deeper in the Spirit, not to burden you or add to your list of activities. Individuals will do the daily contemplative exercises alone, then you will meet as a group to share and encourage.

5. Spend time in conversational prayer. If you have not been praying this way before, it will take some time to feel comfortable. Be patient.

a) You have been having a conversation with God. He is not just now tuning in because you've called His name. You don't need a formal prayer to open the time. Just continue with your conversation in a more reverent mode.

b). Each spoken prayer should be short and on one topic. You don't have to use a different vocabulary with the Father than you do in ordinary conversation.

c) This is a conversation. You may enter into a conversation as many times and whenever you want to.

d) Don't be afraid of silence. Prayer is still going on.

e) Do not take turns praying around the circle. No one has to pray aloud. Anyone can pray at any time.

f) When someone senses that the prayertime is finished, he or she should lead out in a closing prayer, acknowledging God's continuing presence.

Meetings 1 Through 11
Make your times together unstructured and free. Leave room for the Spirit to do exactly what He wants. Plan to discuss the Scripture from the week's devotionals. Use discussion starting questions, such as:

> What did God particularly speak to you about this week?
> How did you observe God's power in your life?
> Were you able to carry the sense of His presence and voice into your daily life? If so, what helped you be able to do it? If you had trouble, what distracted you?
> Which method was especially fruitful for you this week?
> What are your impressions about your experience so far?
> How can we pray for one another this week?

Always have conversational prayertime. It could be in the beginning or at the end. A discussion might bring a need to light and you might stop right then for prayertime. You may have several prayertimes. You will probably change your patterns from week to week as the Spirit flows among you.

Meeting 12
Let this be a time of reflecting over the whole experience and sharing life changes and plans for how to maintain your craving for God. Let participants express appreciation for each other in specific ways. By this time, you will have developed intimacy and will be comfortable praying conversationally. Leave plenty of time in this last gathering to pray.

You might want to continue your journey by using *Secret Place of the Most High: A Journal for Those Who Hunger After the Deep Things of God* by Jennifer Kennedy Dean. Purchase it at your local Christian bookstore or order it by calling 1 (800) 968-7301.

[1]Thomas R. Kelly, *A Testament of Devotion* (New York: Harper and Row, Publishers, 1941), 29.
[2]Jennifer Kennedy Dean, "My One Desire." Copyright 1994, The Praying Life Foundation. Used by permission.

Jennifer Kennedy Dean has become a leader in the study of prayer. Her previous titles include *Heart's Cry* (Principles of Prayer), *The Praying Life: Living Beyond Your Limits,* and *Power Praying: Prayer That Produces Results.* She is also co-founder of the Praying Life Foundation. Through this ministry, Dean conducts international and multidenominational seminars addressing prayer as a relationship rather than an activity. She lives in Blue Springs, Missouri, with her husband, Wayne, and their three sons.